Institute
for
Policy Studies

The Rise and Fall of the 'Soviet Threat':

Domestic Sources of the Cold War Consensus

Alan Wolfe

Institute
for
Policy Studies

The Rise and Fall of the 'Soviet Threat':

Domestic Sources of the Cold War Consensus

Alan Wolfe

The Institute for Policy Studies is a non-partisan research institute. The views expressed in this study are solely those of the author.

Published by the Institute for Policy Studies.

Copies of this book are available from the Institute for Policy Studies, 1901 Q Street, N.W., Washington, D.C. 20009 or Paulus Potterstraat 20, 1071 DA, Amsterdam, Holland.

First Printing: 1979
Library of Congress Catalog Number: 79-919-50
ISBN 0-89758-019-2

C-417

About the Author

Alan Wolfe is currently a Visiting Scholar at the Institute for the Study of Social Change at the University of California, Berkeley. He was previously an associate professor of sociology and political science at Richmond College, City University of New York. Beginning in January, 1980, Dr. Wolfe will serve as associate professor of sociology at Queens College, City University of New York, Flushing.

Alan Wolfe is the author of several books, including *The Seamy Side of Democracy: Repression in America,* for which he was nominated for the Pulitzer Prize in 1973; and *The Limits of Legitimacy: Political Contradictions of Contemporary Capitalism.* Wolfe is widely published in such journals as *Comparative Politics, Social Policy* and *The Nation* on the topics of social democracy and the political forces of liberalism and conservatism in the United States. He continues his research on the resurgence of right-wing politics in the United States, to be published in his forthcoming book, *America's Impasse: The Rise and Decline of Cold War Liberalism.* Dr. Wolfe is a former Visiting Fellow of the Institute for Policy Studies.

Contents

Chapter I:
The Domestic Basis
of the Soviet Threat

"The principal threat to our nation, to world peace, and to the cause of human freedom is the Soviet drive for dominance . . . The Soviet Union has not altered its long-held goal of a world dominated by a single center—Moscow."[1] So spoke an organization called the Committee on the Present Danger, founded in 1976 on the premise that the United States, if it did not build up its defenses, would soon be impotent in the face of Soviet strength. And in speaking, the Committee talked not only for itself, but for an emerging consensus among conservative defense specialists, military planners, and foreign policy experts that a new wave of Soviet aggressiveness was undermining the security of the United States.

Organizations like the Committee on the Present Danger are not a new phenomenon. (Indeed, this Committee borrowed both its name and its purpose from an organization founded in 1950 to warn the United States about the consequences of the Russian detonation of atomic weapons.) From time to time, one or another group of "hard-line" defense specialists has issued chilling reports about the nature of Soviet intentions. There was in 1945 the so-called "long telegram" written by George Kennan from Moscow, which warned State Department officials about an inherent tendency of Russia to expand. There was NSC-68, a 1950 top secret review of Soviet intentions, which prophesied a red future unless the U.S. responded quickly. In 1957, the Gaither Report warned that the U.S. was falling behind the Soviets and needed to regain the initiative. Best-selling books in the late 1950s by Maxwell Taylor and Henry Kissinger warned of America's weakness. More recently, a team of intelligence specialists commissioned by President Ford—called "Team B"—spoke menacingly of a major Soviet military build-up. And, in opposition to President Carter's attempts to win support for a Strategic Arms Limitation Treaty with the Soviet Union, a phalanx of cold war organizations, of which the Committee on the Present Danger is among the more moderate, have sprung into life.

The frequency with which intellectuals and policymakers concern themselves with the Soviet threat raises questions that go to the very heart of America's ability to survive as a democratic

1

society. If the Soviet Union really is a military threat to the American system, then it is impossible to object to taking any and all measures necessary to insure the preservation of the United States. But if the threat is not genuine—if it is exaggerated, distorted, and based upon self-serving needs—then the danger to America's democracy comes as much from within as from without, for in such a case there would be pressure to expand the military budget, curtail basic freedoms, and restrict open access to government on the basis of a premise that was false. It is simply imperative that attempts be made to understand more concretely the role that perceptions of the Soviet Union play in the making of American foreign policy.

Most of the debates taking place about the relative military balance between the Soviet Union and the United States become so technical that only logicians, economists and physicists can follow them. In those discussions, the issue is seen as primarily a *military* one. Whoever has the military advantage, the Committee on the Present Danger claims, has a political advantage as well, for they can use their might to gain influence and territory around the world. The U.S. can combat this Soviet military build-up only with a counter military program of its own.

In this report I will argue that much of the recent hysteria about the Soviet military build-up has much more to do with *domestic* politics than it does with the security of the United States. What is at stake is not who has more arms—both sides have more than enough—but how each superpower perceives the other. And perceptions are determined politically. *I will argue that in the past, U.S. perceptions of hostile Soviet intentions have increased, not when the Russians have become more aggressive or militaristic, but when certain constellations of political forces have come together within the United States to force the question of the Soviet threat onto the American political agenda.* This conclusion, I will try to show, makes the charge that the Soviets have become stronger and more aggressive in recent years inherently dubious. *What explains the extremely negative perceptions of the Soviet Union so popular now in Washington is not the Russian military build-up but the peculiar features of the American political system that will be described in this report.*

The stakes over these questions are high. If the current campaign to convince Americans that they face a clear and present danger from the Soviet Union succeeds, then unity in Washington may be achieved, but at tremendous cost. Alarmism about U.S. national security accelerates military spending, hurts our prosperity, prevents stable prices, erodes gains for minorities and women, reduces popular respect for the rights of other

2

people around the globe, and endangers civil liberties by creating an atmosphere inimical to freedom and diversity. It also endangers peace. A renewed arms race at this particular period, when a new generation of deadly nuclear weapons can be built, would be equal in importance to the U.S. decision to construct the H-bomb. *No question is more important in American politics at this time than how this country decides to view Soviet intentions.*

Every warning about the danger posed by the Soviet Union— after beginning with some thoughts about the advantages of a free society over totalitarianism—resolves itself into two propositions. The first is that the Russians are becoming more aggressive and building up their military might at a more rapid pace. The second is that the United States is becoming weaker, falling behind in military hardware and afraid to show its resolve in a dangerous world.

There is no clear evidence that either proposition is true in the current period. It is an article of faith to the resurgent cold warriors in Washington that the Russians have both expanded the rate of their military build-up and have become more aggressive in their interventions into other countries. The Committee on the Present Danger has called the Soviet military build-up "reminiscent of Nazi Germany's rearmament in the 1930s," a sentiment shared by David C. Jones, Chairman of the Joint Chiefs of Staff; Daniel Graham, a retired Air Force General and cold war activist; and other military specialists.[2] Yet a study undertaken by Congressman Les Aspin, a former Pentagon economist, indicates that any such comparisons to the extremely sharp and rapid Nazi military build-up are inaccurate. Aspin found that "The expansion of Soviet military efforts has been surprisingly steady over time, with some minor fluctuations depending on the stage of weapons development and the deployment cycles the Soviet Union is in."[3] And many other reputable analysts of Soviet behavior agree with Aspin's critique of the Committee on the Present Danger.

Nor is there evidence that America in recent years has become weaker, militarily speaking. It is true that the rate of defense spending in the United States decreased after Vietnam, but, as Aspin points out, while "The Soviets are failing to match our reduction of recent years, . . . they never matched our jumps of previous years."[4] Moreover, in the nuclear age, it is hard to argue that less defense spending makes a country weaker. The weakness of the U.S. was manifest to the world when its defense budgets were exceptionally high during Vietnam. Indeed there is now

3

It is not clear that the Russians have, since 1976, become more "adventuresome" in their foreign interventions, as the Committee on the Present Danger and like-minded groups charge.

evidence, compiled by Philip Morrison and the Boston Study Group, which shows that the U.S. defense posture could be improved by spending *less*.[5] Morrison argues that the huge, highly complex (and very expensive) weapons favored by Pentagon planners are often simply not effective in protecting the American people. Finally, overall levels of military spending are too gross to make conclusions about strength. As many experts have pointed out, the Soviet military establishment is designed for different purposes than that of the U.S., with far more of its budget directed toward internal security and defense.[6]

It is, in addition, not clear that the Russians have, since 1976, become more "adventuresome" in their foreign interventions, as the Committee on the Present Danger and like-minded groups charge. Since the end of World War II, the Soviet Union and the United States have both jockeyed for more favorable positions in the Third World. Sometimes one country gains advantages and sometimes it loses them. In the last few years, according to the resurgent cold warriors, the Soviets have taken the upper hand in this competition; they point to Angola (where Cuban troops were active), Ethiopia, Afghanistan, and Iran as evidence of this new aggression. But the case for a hyperactive Soviet Union simply does not hold. Third World disputes are nearly always local in nature, as the U.S. discovered in Vietnam (and the U.S.S.R. learned in Egypt). Big power intervention by either side can have a temporary effect, but rarely does it have long term significance. Indigenous revolutions have increased in the Third World, but Soviet intervention has not. (These are two different phenomena, although the purveyors of the Soviet threat do not always make this clear.) And, in the final analysis, no country in the world has intervened abroad as many times as the United States.

Finally, the hypothesis that the Soviet Union is becoming more expansionist ignores the overwhelming desire of the Russian leaders to fashion some kind of *modus vivendi* with the United States. Indeed, paralleling the history of the cold war, there has also existed an impressive amount of apparent collaboration between the two superpowers. Each, while formally condemning the belligerence of the other, has recognized separate spheres of interest and has engaged in practical cooperation. Thus, in spite of extreme cold war rhetoric, the U.S. tacitly acknowledged Soviet control over Eastern Europe in the 1940s, did not support the Hungarian revolt in the 1950s, and accepted the Soviet's drive for nuclear parity in the 1960s and 1970s. Likewise the Russians, over and above their anti-capitalist ideology, declined to sign a separate peace treaty with East Germany, backed down over Cuba, and agreed not to challenge directly the U.S. bombing of their allies in Southeast Asia. In acts, if not always in speech, each superpower has recognized that it shares an interest with the other in preserving a world order from would-be challengers.[7]

This search for accommodation between the two superpowers means that often they act in a less hostile manner than their rhetoric suggests. In recent years, for example, the Russians have bent over backwards to obtain a SALT treaty, refusing to break off negotiations when the Americans changed the terms of the discussion early in the Carter Administration. They agreed to Mutual and Balanced Force Reduction (MBFR) talks in Vienna at a time when the U.S. was considering unilateral troop withdrawals, hardly evidence of a desire to split the Atlantic Alliance or to overrun Western Europe. In the last Geneva talks about the Middle East before Camp David they were quite accommodating. They sought to preserve detente even while the U.S. broke all international rules of proper conduct in its bombing of Cambodia. If the extreme anti-Soviet views are correct, it becomes difficult to understand Russian eagerness for wheat deals, most favored nation trading status, cooperation in space, and other evidence of mutual support between the countries.

Thus, substantial evidence points to the conclusion that one cannot properly conclude that the Soviets are becoming stronger and more aggressive while the U.S. is becoming weaker and more cowardly. And if this is true of the present period, it is also true of the past, where the passage of time has enabled observers to determine whether the predictions made about future build-ups would turn out to be true. George Kistiakowsky, former science advisor to President Eisenhower, has argued that every significant attempt to compare Soviet and American military strength in the past has exaggerated the power of the former country and the weakness of the latter.[8] For this reason, Kistiakowsky argues that there is at least *prima facie* evidence for being suspicious about the current concern among conservatives about an expanded military build-up on the part of the Soviet Union.

The failure of these warnings about the imminence of the Soviet threat to correspond to what was actually taking place in the real world gives credence to the notion that domestic politics may have more to do with the rise and fall of anti-Soviet sentiment than international conflict. *When different interpretations of Soviet behavior are equally feasible, what factors combine to give the most negative interpretation the greatest currency within the United States?*

In this study I will try to answer this question. While it is true that an anti-communist consensus has existed in the United States since 1945, the degree of anti-Soviet hostility has had peaks and valleys. By identifying what those peak periods were, it becomes possible to see whether each peak period contains certain political similarities. I will argue that five common features run through each period in which anti-Soviet perceptions manifestly increased: a disequilibrium in party politics; the existence of serious threats to the hegemony of the executive branch of government; an outbreak of a serious case of inter-service rivalry; the development of a strong conflict within the foreign policy establishment over the proper focal points of American policy; and the coming to power of political coalitions organized around a need to spur economic growth. There is strong evidence, I will conclude, that the opposition to the SALT II treaty and the new cold war militancy in Washington have more to do with the domestic politics of the late 1970s than they do with the Soviet military build-up, or indeed with international politics at all.

Chapter II:
Three Peaks of Hostility

The U.S. and the Soviet Union, although allies during World War II, have been wary of each other since the Russian Revolution. This wariness broke out into active hostility when World War II ended, and it has continued ever since. Nonetheless, in spite of a constant fear of the Soviet Union in American politics since 1946, it is possible to identify differences in the way that the Soviet threat has been perceived for the past thirty-five years. In an influential study of the cold war, for example, Daniel Yergin has made a distinction between what he calls the "Riga axioms" and the "Yalta axioms" about Soviet conduct. The former takes the view that the Soviets are inherently bent on expansion, that the danger they pose constantly grows, and therefore that only firm U.S. resolve can meet the threat. (Yergin adopts the term Riga from the Latvian city from which Americans observed Soviet conduct before the U.S. recognized the regime.) The latter view, named after the city in which Roosevelt, Stalin, and Churchill achieved an understanding on the nature of the postwar world, sees the Soviets as a serious rival, but one that demands diplomatic responses through which each power tries to accommodate the interests of the other. The difference between the two interpretations is not that one is more sympathetic than the other to the Russians—both view the Soviet Union as an antagonist—but that the Riga position implies a military response, while the Yalta axioms do not make conflict the litmus test of U.S.-Soviet relations.[9]

Yergin's distinction is helpful in charting the rise and fall of the Soviet threat in American politics since the end of World War II. There have been certain periods of time in which, although much attention was paid to the evils of communism, the U.S. did not actively pursue a directly provocative course with respect to Russia. And there have been other times when a concern with Soviet perceptions of American weakness have led to a veritable obsession with "standing up to the Russians." One must distinguish between a long term secular trend—in which hostility toward the Russians has clearly declined since the late 1940s—and periodic cycles during the course of the trend, when anti-Soviet perceptions sharply increase and then subside.

For purposes of this study, a high peak in the perception of the Soviet threat can be defined as having the following characteristics. First, some important group of policymakers, in an official or quasi-official forum, issues a report making a claim that the Russians are getting stronger and the Americans weaker. This report is then read and debated in the highest circles of policymaking, fashioning a new consensus about the Soviet danger. As a result of the new perception, certain steps are taken to demonstrate America's concern. The two most important indications of the new mood are a decision to increase the defense budget and a decision to demonstrate U.S. strength in some way, either through a direct intervention or through a symbolic display like moving the American fleet. Both kinds of action are meant by policymakers to prove American resolve. Therefore, a peak in the perception of the Soviet threat requires a conjuncture of an ideological offensive (as manifested in some new official statement about the rivalry between the two superpowers) combined with a manifest shift in policy toward policies that tangibly demonstrate a firmer course.

Contrariwise, a valley in the perception of the Soviet threat would occur when either the ideology or the action was missing, or both. For example, if the actual defense budget remains constant or decreases, and at the same time if the actual number of times that the U.S. "shows the fleet" declines, then such a period would not be an anti-Soviet peak, even if the ideological hostility toward the Soviet Union was strong. For our purposes, a trough in the hostile perception of the Soviet Union will be considered a period in which an anti-Russian ideology did not correspond with a palpable rise in foreign policy belligerence to produce a new U.S. offensive in the world.

Based upon these criteria, postwar American policy has gone through two peaks, two valleys, and now seems to be entering a third peak. These periods can be identified as follows:

1. *The first peak:* the period of the cold war initiation. Right after World War II ended until the early 1950s, a very negative interpretation of Soviet conduct began to win out in the United States. As a result, the basic decisions that began the cold war—such as developing the H-bomb—were made.

2. *The first valley:* the Eisenhower retrenchment. In spite of all the anti-communist rhetoric of John Foster Dulles, ideology did not correspond with action under Eisenhower. The defense budget did not increase and U.S. foreign policy actions designed to prove America's resolve to the Russians were relatively few.

3. *The second peak:* the cold war consolidation. Beginning in the late 1950s with the Gaither Report, a number of defense specialists began to question the Eisenhower approach. The anti-Soviet ideology was carried forward but to it was added,

especially between 1961 and 1962, a new American belligerence in foreign affairs, culminating in the Cuban Missile Crisis.

4. *The second valley:* detente. Starting fitfully in 1963 with Kennedy's American University speech and continuing into the Nixon Administration, big-power cooperation began to increase. By the mid-1970s, the defense budget (as a percent of GNP) had decreased, foreign interventions, while more blatant, were less numerous, and SALT I was signed and ratified.

5. *The third peak:* the anti-SALT II campaign. Since 1976, a new wave of anti-Soviet hysteria has broken out. Although President Carter has tried to resist parts of it, he has also shown himself amenable to other parts. U.S. interventions have not resumed, but increases in the defense budget have. The nature of this period is not yet clear, but there is a strong possibility that it may emerge into a peak of anti-Soviet perception, especially if the SALT II treaty fails to be ratified. But even if the treaty passes, the new round of defense spending necessary to win votes could equally spur a revival of the Soviet threat.

By reviewing the features of each of these periods in greater detail, it becomes possible to see what the peak points have in common—and what differentiates them from the valleys—in order to begin to unravel the domestic factors that combine to produce extreme domestic perceptions of the Soviet threat within the United States.

The Cold War Begins (1948-1952)

The issue that dominated policy discussions within the United States after World War II ended involved more than anything else the correct *perception* that the U.S. should have of Russian behavior. When the Yalta agreements called for free elections in Eastern Europe at the earliest possible time, for example, Stalin interpreted it to mean that the Soviets would be allowed a free hand in Poland, whereas Americans were sure that it meant that the future of that country was up for grabs. The Yalta agreement, as Truman's chief of staff Admiral William Leahy pointed out, "was susceptible to two interpretations."[10] As Stalin moved to consolidate Soviet control over Poland, the question became which interpretation would be the official American position: was Stalin's move to be perceived as acceptable under Yalta, or as the breaking of a treaty requiring a firm American response?

Secretary of War Henry L. Stimson and General George Marshall argued that the U.S. should be cautious in interpreting Stalin's moves because Russian cooperation was essential to the

United States. Truman rejected that advice and turned instead to Leahy, whose antipathy toward the Russians was well known. Leahy called a meeting of high State Department officials known to be hostile to Stimson's and Marshall's interpretation of Soviet conduct. "It was the consensus of opinion of the conferees," Leahy wrote in his diary, "that the time had arrived to take a strong American attitude toward the Soviets, and that no particular harm can now be done to our war prospects even if Russia should slow down or even stop its war effort in Europe and Asia."[11] Having thus chosen a negative interpretation of Soviet behavior, Truman met with Soviet Ambassador Molotov and proceeded to abuse him (and his country) verbally. "I have never been talked to like that in my life," Molotov exclaimed. "Carry out your agreements and you won't get talked to like that," was Truman's response.[12]

Hostility toward the Russian ambassador, however, was not something around which a diplomatic policy could be built. Policies are based, not only on the actions of other countries, but on how those actions are interpreted. The importance of the 1946-50 period was that, whenever it mattered, the U.S. opted for an interpretation that emphasized the globally aggressive character of the Soviet Union over equally plausible interpretations that stressed the other country's more narrow pursuit of a limited self-interest.

For example, when Truman sent Harry Hopkins—Roosevelt's most trusted advisor—to Moscow in the summer of 1945, Stalin was found to be reasonable, interested in possible attempts at cooperation, and even willing to compromise over Poland. The discussions were so frank and open that the two countries began to feel that they understood each other much better. This understanding continued for a time after Truman appointed James F. Byrnes as his Secretary of State. Conservative, Southern, Irish Catholic, and relentlessly ambitious, Byrnes felt that an accommodation with the Russians made good political sense. While in Moscow in late 1945, he negotiated a compromise with Stalin over Eastern Europe, won agreement for a United Nations Atomic Energy Commission, and worked out plans for Asia. There seemed to be no question that diplomacy with the Russians worked as diplomacy generally works: slowly, compromisingly, ambiguously, and peacefully. Yet all this evidence of the possibility of cooperation with the Soviet Union would be ignored as American politics turned increasingly in a cold war direction.

Obvious points of tension and disagreement existed between the Russians and the Americans over such matters as Trieste,

In spite of the broad domestic coalition that was finding coherence around the notion of a Soviet threat, the idea of Russian expansionism was not immediately accepted, either within the elite or among the general population.

Iran, and reparations. Distinguished Americans like Marshall, Stimson, Hopkins, and Byrnes had all shown that it was possible to resolve some of those tensions through diplomacy. But within the United States a different lesson was being emphasized. Rejecting all evidence to the contrary, influential individuals and organizations began to argue that tension was the rule and cooperation the exception. The Russians, it was claimed, were an aggressive and totalitarian power bent on world conquest, and their ambitious schemes could be foiled only by American resolve. If Stalin refused to negotiate, that proved the point. And if he did, it merely showed how untrustworthy he was. Constructing a mindset from which all evidence could be shaped to fit their negative image of the Soviet Union, these officials were successful at undermining the efforts of Stimson and Byrnes. A hardline position began to emerge at home.

One faction that was instrumental in solidifying the hardline was the Russian desk of the State Department. For years Russian affairs had been in the hands of a generation of would-be patricians who aped the crumbling aristocracy of Europe. Joseph Grew, Loy Henderson, Eldridge Dubrow and others—all of them pompous, anti-semetic, tolerant of Hitler, elitist, anti-democratic, and ultrareactionary in their politics—used every opportunity at their command to win a confused Truman around to their hardline views on the Soviet Union.[13]

Truman was receptive to the anti-Soviet views of the State Department. But those views became dominant only because a number of groups were willing to listen to extreme denunciations of Soviet conduct for their own reasons. Prominent Democrats like W. Averill Harriman and Dean Acheson were convinced that a firm anti-Soviet position would counter the vulnerability of their party in the conservative environment of the postwar period. Representatives of the Navy and the Air Force, trying to gain bureaucratic turf for themselves, saw in the Soviet threat a chance to score points against the Army. Liberals in the labor movement saw an opportunity to gain respectability and to wage war at the same time against radical antagonists, many of whom belonged to the Communist Party and thus could be painted with the anti-Russian brush. Industrialists with pro-European inclinations saw a chance to forge a close alliance between Germany—just recently the enemy—and the United States. Keynesian economists thought that the high military budgets associated with the Soviet threat would continue economic recovery and avoid another depression. In short, domestic interests were coalescing in such a way as to give currency to an extremely reactionary view of Soviet intentions that gained force and momentum due to factors above and beyond what the Soviets were doing.

In spite of the broad domestic coalition that was finding coherence around the notion of a Soviet threat, the idea of Russian expansionism was not immediately accepted, either within the elite or among the general population. Skeptics had to be converted by a sustained campaign to win support for one particular, and highly biased, interpretation of Soviet motives. Initially George Kennan, a career diplomat and the State Department's leading expert on Russia, took the lead in developing this point of view. First in a long telegram from Moscow and then in a 1945 article published under the name of "Mr. X" in the semi-official journal, *Foreign Affairs,* Kennan argued that Soviet imperialism was based on the Russian national character. If Kennan was correct in his analysis, then no compromise with the Soviets was possible, for they would not be satisfied until their way of life prevailed throughout the world. Kennan later came to regret the monomaniacal view of Soviet intentions that shaped U.S. policies, but he clearly bore some responsibility for it, since his analysis left policymakers little option but to take the most anti-Soviet position possible. Kennan would not be the last policymaker who used anti-Soviet rhetoric only to be overtaken by more extreme positions that left him isolated.

The crest of anti-Soviet thinking in this initial wave of belligerence took the form of a study group organized by the Departments of Defense and State in 1949 to ponder the implications of Soviet possession of the atomic bomb. Eventually producing a position paper for use within the National Security Council called NSC-68, the study group painted a horrifying picture of Soviet desires. The nub of the argument was that an unbreakable connection existed between totalitarian conditions at home and an expansionist foreign policy abroad. "The Kremlin's policy toward areas not under its control is the elimination of resistance to its will and the extension of its

12

influence and control. It is driven to follow this policy because it cannot . . . tolerate the existence of free societies; to the Kremlin the most mild and inoffensive free society is an affront, a challenge and a subversive influence. Given the nature of the Kremlin, and the evidence at hand, it seems clear that the ends toward which this policy is directed are the same as those where its control has already been established."[14] NSC-68, in other words, denied that the Russians could ever act like all other big powers, seeking to maximize their strength in some places and minimize their losses in others. Diplomacy means choice; by that definition, diplomacy with the Soviet Union was out of the question because they could never choose—their internal character would drive them to expand everywhere. NSC-68 analyzed Russian intentions in terms of a model of totalitarianism based on Nazi Germany. That the Soviet Union was a different social system in a different historical period was a distinction passed over by the emerging anti-Soviet consensus.

NSC-68 was never officially adopted by the Truman Administration, but it is generally viewed as a turning point in American policy because it provided the rationale for two major transformations. First, it called for programs which would triple the defense budget. Spurred by the Korean War, the defense budget did, in fact, shoot up. And since much of the newly expended money went to Europe, upon which NSC-68 had concentrated, and not Asia, where the war was actually taking place, the authors of the document were vindicated. Second, NSC-68 had a major impact, if an indirect one, on public opinion. Although it was a highly classified document seen only by a few, its intention, in the words of Dean Acheson, "was to bludgeon the mass mind of 'top government' so that not only could the President make a decision but that the decision could be carried out."[15] After NSC-68, dissenters within the Establishment who wished to articulate an alternative view of Soviet intentions had a far more difficult time winning a hearing. Now more united, the elite would convey the impression of the Soviet threat with greater clarity to the American people.

Thus, the period between the end of World War II and 1952 qualifies as a peak in anti-Soviet hostility because it meets the two criteria outlined above. First, an ideological offensive was undertaken against the Russians, one that emphasized the most negative features of Soviet activities in an ambiguous context. And second, this ideological offensive was combined with a more active foreign policy stance, particularly in an increase in defense spending oriented toward Western Europe.

An Official Perception of the Soviet Union:

The Kremlin regards the United States as the only major threat to the achievement of its fundamental design. There is a basic conflict between the idea of freedom under a government of laws, and the idea of slavery under the grim oligarchy of the Kremlin, which has come to a crisis with the polarization of power described in Section I, and the exclusive possession of atomic weapons by the two protagonists. The idea of freedom, moreover, is peculiarly and intolerably subversive of the idea of slavery. But the opposite is not true. The implacable purpose of the slave state to eliminate the challenge of freedom has placed the two great powers at opposite poles. It is this fact which gives the present polarization of power the quality of crisis.

This statement, and many others like it that are contained in NSC-68, indicates that to the men who wrote this document, there was a direct relationship between the authoritarian internal structure of a state and an external desire to expand. This notion, still advanced by anti-Soviet thinkers, is simply not true. Some democratic states have been highly expansionist, and some authoritarian ones (like Franco's Spain) have preoccupied themselves at home. Generally, states will become more active in foreign policy depending on their power in the world, not on their internal structure.

Retrenchment (1952-1957)

By 1950, a new hostile view of Russian conduct had emerged within U.S. policymaking circles. Yet even though the Soviet Union had replaced Nazi Germany in the American mind as the enemy, there still were significant obstacles to the adoption of the world view laid out in NSC-68. For one thing, most Americans thought of themselves as a peaceful people and were not prepared to engage their hearts and minds in a perpetual war after just having completed a global one. In addition, a state of vigilance against Soviet expansion required high defense budgets, which meant increased taxes, and Americans have never particularly liked to pay taxes. Finally, cold war anxieties carried with them a domestic state of emergency, strong presidential powers, and an atmosphere of crisis—none of which seemed compatible with the overwhelming desire for normalcy in the postwar atmosphere. By electing General Eisenhower president, the American people selected a man who was not so prone to extreme interpretations of the Soviet threat. By 1952, the peak was turning into a valley, and a period of retrenchment began.

Eisenhower's Administration, like all of them in the postwar period, was staunchly anti-communist. The new Secretary of State, John Foster Dulles, was unbending in his opposition to communism, the kind of man who opposed sending a prefunctory telegram to the Russians on Stalin's death for fear that it might be interpreted as an incitement to revolution.[16] Dulles' self-righteous zeal colored the rhetoric of the Eisenhower Administration, but it did not control its policies. The fiscal conservatism of the Republican Party continuously acted as a constraint on U.S. policy during the 1950s, for any increase in defense spending was considered intolerable. Forced to practice what he called "maximum protection at bearable cost,"[17] Dulles was hamstrung in operationalizing some of his more extreme views. In the end, just six months from his death, even Dulles seemed to have second thoughts about his more inflexible notions. In mid-1958 he explored the idea of a partial military disengagement in Europe and seemed to endorse a reduction in tensions with the Russians.[18]

Thus, although the Eisenhower Administration possessed an ideological hatred of communism, it declined to mobilize an aggressive foreign policy against the Russians. (Anti-communism and anti-Soviet perceptions are not the same thing. Dulles, for example, seemed to be more hostile to the Chinese than the Russians, while some current anti-Soviet belligerents— like Zbigniew Brzezinski and James Schlesinger—are willing to form an alliance with a communist country like China.) For this reason, the Eisenhowever Administration was missing one of the two elements that constitutes an extreme peak of anti-Soviet perceptions.

Neither an increase in defense spending nor an active interventionary stance designed to prove America's resolve characterized Eisenhower's foreign policy *actions*. In defense policy, the Administration repudiated the doctrines of NSC-68 and developed what it called the "New Look" in military strategy. The New Look, as Samuel Huntington pointed out, "was the special reflection of the values and goals of Dwight Eisenhower, George Humphrey, John Foster Dulles, Arthur W. Radford, their associates in the Administration, and the dominant groups in the Republican Party."[19] For this reason, it sought "stability of expenditures,"[20] not vast increases in new weapons systems.

A Russian Looks at Dulles:

A word about Dulles. Dulles often said that the goal of the United States was to push Socialism in Europe back to the borders of the Soviet Union, and he seemed to be obsessed with the idea of encirclement. He extended America's economic embargo of the Soviet Union to include a boycott on cultural exchange. Not even Soviet tourists and chess players were permitted to visit the United States. I remember, too, that when the U.S. sponsored some sort of international convention of chess our own delegation wasn't allowed to attend.

However, I'll say this for him: Dulles knew how far he could push us, and he never pushed us too far. For instance, when the forces of our two countries confronted each other in the Near East during the events in Syria and Lebanon in 1958, Dulles stepped back from the brink of war. The reactionary forces of the United States and England pulled back their troops, partly as a result of Dulles' prudence. The prestige of the Soviet Union was enhanced in all the progressive countries of the world.

When Dulles died, I told my friends that although he had been a man who lived and breathed hatred of Communism and who despised progress, he had never stepped over that brink which he was always talking about in his speeches; and for that reason alone we should lament his passing.

From *Khrushchev Remembers*

Under enormous pressure from anti-Soviet idealogues, Eisenhower, as Huntington notes, held the line remarkably well; it was not until the very end of his administration that the defense budget began to rise.

Nor, in this period of retrenchment, was there a significant increase in symbolic demonstrations of American power. Overall, Eisenhower's administration saw a greater number of foreign policy adventures than Truman's (57 in 8 years, or an average of 7.1 per year, compared to Truman's 35 in 6 years, for an average of 5.8 per year) but a much lower number than Kennedy and Johnson (88 in 8 years, or an average of 11.0 per year).[21] But the majority of these actions were not big power confrontations; they were more old-style interventions to help specific business interests (as in Guatemala) than new-style interventions designed to prove to the Russians that the U.S. was willing to flex its muscles. The Eisenhower people did not make every Third World revolution a "test of will" as the Kennedy team would do. Some of the major foreign policy problems of the Eisenhower period did not directly involve a U.S.-Soviet confrontation, especially the British attempt to hold on to the Suez Canal. Moreover, in spite of vast turmoil against Soviet rule in Eastern Europe, the Administration took no major steps to destabilize Russian power.

For these reasons, the anti-Soviet activists who had written NSC-68 became extremely disenchanted with the Eisenhower Administration, especially in the beginning of its second term. They began to organize themselves for a new offensive in developing a negative perception of Soviet conduct. There followed a second peak in cold war hostility as they came closer to holding power.

Cold War consolidation (1957-1963)

The second peak in anti-Soviet sentiment began to form, as had the first, around a top secret review of Soviet capabilities. Called the "Gaither Report" after the review committee chairman, H. Rowan Gaither, *Deterrence and Survival in the Nuclear Age* reaffirmed the consensus that had been formed with NSC-68.[22] A simple chart captured the message of the report. With Soviet efforts plotted in a thick black line and the U.S. capacity in a thin one, the chart showed the U.S. ahead in the early 1950s, equality at the time the report was issued (1957) and a projected Soviet lead for the future. The Report also contained a point that would come back to haunt American policymakers; the authors claimed (falsely) that the Soviets soon would have enough intercontinental ballistic missiles to overwhelm America's defenses. In the strongest possible terms, the Report urged an immediate turn to high defense budgets and an effort to indoctrinate the public into a crisis mentality.

The Gaither Report was only one of the attacks on Eisenhower's New Look. Former Army Chief of Staff Maxwell Taylor (see Chapter V) led the public barrage with his book *An Uncertain Trumpet*, in which he called for a strategy of "Flexible Response" that, by building up conventional arms, would permit the U.S. to wield its forces more effectively.[23] The Council on Foreign Relations had sponsored a study by Henry Kissinger that argued much the same thesis, and also advocated planning

Past and Projected Relationship Between U.S. and U.S.S.R. Military Effort

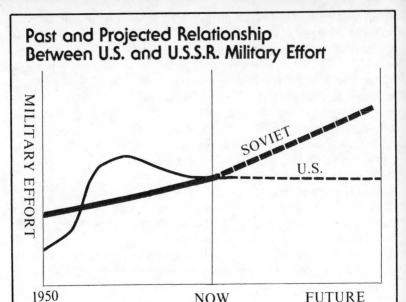

MILITARY EFFORT

SOVIET

U.S.

1950   NOW   FUTURE

From: *The Gaither Report* (1957). The interesting point to note about this chart is that, even though it symbolized the kind of thinking that would have an enormous impact on U.S. defense policy, whoever drew the diagram would have failed an introductory course in policy analysis or economics. There are no figures given, the dates are vague, and the lines in the chart do not measure any empirical reality. In other words, the purposes of the chart were much more political than analytical. Nonetheless, it is a sign of the hysteria of the times that a chart this analytically weak could be taken seriously by anybody. It was the top secret nature of the Gaither Report that enabled such irresponsibility to take place.

for "limited nuclear war" so that the U.S. would not be bound by Dulles' reliance on big bombs.[24] Ambitious Democratic senators—like Stuart Symington of Missouri, John Kennedy of Massachusetts, Lyndon Johnson of Texas, and Hubert Humpheyy of Minnesota (all of them candidates for president in 1960)—were attracted by the new wave of anti-Soviet sentiment, seeing in it a relatively safe way to criticize Eisenhower's complacency. If any of these men were elected president in 1960 a more active U.S. stance in the world and higher military budgets would have been sure to follow.

Kennedy, the winner in this scramble, did not wait long. In his first year in office he increased the defense budget by 15%, putting most of the money into combat-related operations like Army divisions, the Marine Corps, and active vessels. He tripled draft calls, asked for the power to call up the reserves, and supported a civil defense program as a response to an announcement by Nikita Khrushchev that he was increasing Russia's defense budget. Paul Nitze and other authors of both NSC-68 and the Gaither Report were given high policymaking positions in the State and Defense Departments. Ignoring Eisenhower's by now legendary warning about a military-industrial complex whose "total influence . . . is felt in every city, every state house, every office of the federal government," Kennedy gave free rein to his new Secretary of Defense Robert S. McNamara to make America's military might more "usable," that is, more able to be moved around the world to demonstrate America's willingness to control world events. (His support for "Special Forces" to be engaged in counter-insurgency warfare was a manifestation of this.) He let it be known that he would welcome a head-to-head confrontation with the Soviet Union, something that Eisenhower had tried to avoid. The cold war was back, and in its revivified form, it was more confrontational.[25]

None of Kennedy's activism would have been possible without rekindling the image of the Soviet menace. Dean Rusk, the new Secretary of State, not only adopted Eisenhower's off-the-cuff remark about falling dominoes, but seemed to make it a principle of national policy. From now on, every conflict in the world, regardless of how far from home, would be seen as a supreme test of American resolve in the face of communist "aggression." (Rusk even linked Russia together with China, while a more perceptive statesman would have tried to exploit their differences.) A meeting with Khrushchev at Vienna produced no breakthroughs and was unable to patch up the hostility caused by the infamous U-2 incident. In the hostile world atmosphere that was the logical result of his "get tough" stance, Kennedy acted belligerently in Berlin (contributing to the construction of a wall that he was unable to remove), upped the U.S. commitment in Southeast Asia with consequences that would prove disastrous for the United States, and eschewed diplomacy over missiles in Cuba for a confrontation that left the whole world breathless with fear. Within two years, Kennedy had faced more foreign policy "crises" than faced Eisenhower in all eight of his presidential years.[26]

If evidence had existed that the Soviet Union had become palpably more aggressive, Kennedy's intensification of the Soviet threat might have been justified. But the evidence, as it usually is, was ambiguous. There can be little doubt that to at least some degree Khrushchev was testing the new president with bluffs and boasts. But boasting is not policy. If anything, Soviet foreign policy seemed to have become even more conservative since the death of Stalin. His first successor, Georgi Malenkov, tried to downplay military affairs in order to increase consumer spending within the Soviet Union. Even though Khrushchev played upon Russian military opposition to this approach to win their support, once in power he continued to favor an expansion of consumer goods. (The Russian leaders, like their American counterparts, have to worry about their popularity.) In 1956, Khrushchev repudiated Stalinism and relaxed Russia's hold over Yugoslavia and other Eastern European countries, though as those countries took advantage of their new found freedom, he backed off and reimposed Soviet control. Apart from the Soviet Union's blatant attempt to maintain its political control over Eastern Europe, its foreign policy was characterized by attempts to curry favor with the newly independent countries of the Third World (although it was not sure how) and a zig-zag between trying to find some sort of big-power cooperation with the United States and attempting to tweak its nose.

But despite such contradictory evidence of Soviet behavior, the new belligerents that came to power with Kennedy chose to ignore all evidence that did not conform to their fairly set view of Soviet expansionism. Their notion of a "missile gap"—which Kennedy had used effectively in his campaign—proved to be a lie; the Russians had less than a handful of ICBMs (one hand, not two) in 1960. Khrushchev had been bluffing, and moreover he was able to carry out his bluff over his own cold warriors by citing exaggerated U.S. estimates of Soviet strength. (We don't need any more, he told his generals, for look how many they say we already have.)[27]

Moreover, as was the case with the authors of NSC-68, the new cold warriors had a perception of Soviet intentions that was consistently negative. Refusing to understand the Soviet Union as a great power trying to maximize its interests in a world of great powers, they ignored nuance, took literally statements made for internal Soviet consumption, and tried their best to fit every Soviet action into a theory of communist expansion, whether the action had anything to do with the theory or not. Finally, the Kennedy men ignored evidence of internal splits within the socialist camp—such as the defection of Yugoslavia and the coming defection of China—because their mindset would not let them see its significance.

There is reason to believe that before he died, John Kennedy had come to understand the folly of his hard-line anti-Soviet

How to be More Dialectical Than the Marxists

The Soviet Union watched the arrival of the new administration with marked interest. Khrushchev, who had given up on Eisenhower after the U-2 incident and the collapse of the Paris summit in May 1960, seized several opportunities to semaphore his hopes for Kennedy. His messages to Harriman and others after the election were followed by a Pugwash meeting on disarmament in Moscow in December. These gatherings, so called because they began with a conference called for the Cleveland financier, Cyrus Eaton, at his summer place in Pugwash, Nova Scotia, brought together disarmament experts from both sides in supposedly unoffical exchanges. Walt Rostow and Jerome B. Wiesner, who were among the Americans at the Moscow meeting, saw V.V. Kuznetsov of the Soviet Foreign Office and urged the release of two American RB-47 fliers, shot down over the Arctic the preceeding July. In the course of their talk Kuznetsov mentioned the campaign furore about a 'missile gap' and suggested that, if the new administration went in for massive rearmament, it could not expect the Russians to sit still. Rostow replied that any Kennedy rearmament would be designed to improve the stability of the deterrent, and that the Soviet Union should recognize this as in the interests of peace; but Kuznetsov, innocent of the higher calculus of deterrence as recently developed in the United States, brusquely dismissed the explanation.

From Arthur Schlesinger, Jr., *A Thousand Days*

This passage perhaps says more about how Kennedy's advisors viewed Soviet credulity than it does about Soviet intentions.

position. In an unusually reasonable speech at American University on June 10, 1963, he spoke a new language, one stressing a search for areas of cooperation with the Soviet Union. He then forcibly pushed through Congress a test-ban treaty with the Russians which not only halted poisoning of the environment but also constituted a significant political defeat for dyed-in-the-wool cold warriors, who opposed the treaty until the end.

Kennedy seemed to be making an effort to back down from the confrontation mentality that had brought him serious embarrassment in the Bay of Pigs invasion. By 1963, the second wave of anti-Soviet belligerency seemed to be coming to an end.

Yet although Kennedy did take a few courageous steps to bring the cold war under control, he also began the process that ultimately led to a U.S. defeat in Indochina. Both Kennedy and his successor Lyndon Johnson were determined not to expose themselves to the right-wing charge of being soft on communism. Accepting at face value the notion of an international communist conspiracy, they trapped themselves by their own rhetoric. Their view of the world made them escalate a nationalist struggle for independence in Vietnam into a major confrontation with both the Soviet Union and China, neither of which wanted it. China, as events would show, has traditionally been at odds with Vietnam. And the Russians, while supplying Vietnam with arms and with political support in the international arena, did everything they could to bring the war to an end, for they wanted above all else to stabilize the area. By the way it intervened in Vietnam, the U.S. was creating a self-fulfilling prophecy, forcing the socialist bloc countries to oppose its moves, thereby confirming American suspicion of Russian and Chinese "intransigence."

The period between 1957 and 1962 constitutes the second peak of anti-Soviet concern because it combined a new ideological offensive—the Gaither Report and the Taylor and Kissinger books—with deliberate actions like raising the military budget and increasing the number of direct U.S. foreign policy actions. Although nostalgia about the Kennedy presidency has somewhat obscured the fact, this period was also a time of extreme cold war tension in the everyday lives of ordinary people: crises, civil defense, and brinks of terror. The Kennedy-Johnson Administrations were sympathetic to some of the most extreme anti-Soviet views floating around Washington and made them rationales for American policy.

Detente (1963-64; 1968-78)

The second peak had crested early with Kennedy's American University speech and attempts to negotiate a test-ban treaty, but because of the persistence of the war in Vietnam, a full-scale relaxation of tensions was impossible to achieve. It was not until the Nixon years that detente would become a reality.

Nixon's was hardly a pacifist administration. In his conduct of the war in Southeast Asia, as a recent book by William

22

Nixon's 1972 China trip marked a watershed in U.S. politics, for it brought to an end America's longstanding attempt to pretend that the world's largest country did not exist.

Shawcross demonstrates, Nixon (and Kissinger) acted with extreme insensitivity, cruelty, and ignorance.[28] Moreover, both were adept at manipulating anti-communist symbols when it suited them to do so. Nonetheless, Nixon did begin to take the steps that would prove to the world that big-power politics works more effectively in the international system than ideological rigidity. In spite of the extreme anti-Soviet views of his Secretary of Defense James Schlesinger, Nixon's policies of detente with the Russians and his opening with China meant that the cold war could not be carried on as it had been.

Nixon's 1972 China trip marked a watershed in U.S. politics, for it brought to an end America's longstanding attempt to pretend that the world's largest country did not exist. But from the point of view of anti-Soviet perceptions, it did not constitute a relaxation of tensions, for it could be interpreted as an anti-Soviet move. More significant for U.S.-Russian relations was the negotiation of the Strategic Arms Limitation Treaty (over the opposition of Democratic hard-liners). Nixon, even more remarkably, won approval for the SALT I treaty in the Senate and managed to have its provisions accepted by the Pentagon.[29] While it is certainly true that the SALT I treaty legitimated the arms race by creating high ceilings which each side then felt obligated to fill, there can also be no doubt that its approval meant a modification of the pattern of mutual antagonism between the U.S. and the Soviet Union. In this sense the most important product of detente was the intangible one, the sense that it was possible for two superpowers to find concrete areas of agreement so that each could look more at its own society rather than blaming the other for its problems. For this reason alone, Nixon accomplished more toward the relaxation of anti-Soviet perceptions than his Democratic predecessors.

Behind foreign policy decisions there generally lies a theory about nation states and how they behave. The cold war had been motivated by a theory that had taken hold in policymaking circles which argued that because Russia was a totalitarian society, it was bound to expand as much as possible, forcing the

U.S. to "contain" it (the Riga axioms). In order to bring about detente, Nixon and Kissinger were forced to discard this theory in favor of a "Yalta" mentality that would rationalize big power politics. It is worth a short digression to consider their approach.

Kissinger, schooled in the Germanic tradition of political theory, understood that power is inherently conservative. Leaders of countries (and of organizations), he believed, try to protect their privileged position and are inherently suspicious of any challenges to their authority. From this point of view, Kissinger quickly recognized that, whatever their respective ideologies, the U.S. and the Soviet Union were both powerful states that would operate as conservative forces in the world. Both had an interest in protecting themselves from challenges, whether (of concern to the Americans) from other capitalist countries like Germany, or (of concern to the Russians) from other socialist countries like China, or (of concern to both) from instability in the Third World. Kissinger argued that although there were many possible centers of power in the Third World, the U.S. and the Soviet Union together were so overwhelmingly powerful militarily that they could insure "stability." Rather than worrying about Soviet intentions—which in Kissinger's view just "confuse[s] the debate"—the U.S. should "discipline power so that it bears a rational relationship to the objectives likely to be in dispute."[30] While willing to bring up the Soviet threat for domestic purposes, Kissinger was not fixated on it.

These views were not necessarily "better" or more "moral" than those of the anti-Soviet hawks, but they were different. The clear import of Kissinger's *realpolitik* meant an end to the excessive ideological hostility between the two superpowers, and therefore fewer attempts to mobilize America's force around the world.

By the two measures being used in this study to represent foreign policy aggressiveness—increases in the defense budget and the number of shows of force—the Nixon period constituted a definite valley. Expenditures on national defense as a percentage of the Gross National Product showed the following pattern in the 1960s and 1970s:[31]

1966	8.0%	1971	6.60%
1967	8.98	1972	6.27
1968	8.85	1973	5.63
1969	8.16	1974	5.45
1970	7.48	1975	5.49
		1976	5.09

In short, fairly dramatic decreases in the percentage of GNP consumed by the defense budget took place under Nixon. Moreover, there was a similar drop in the number of foreign policy interventions. Although the Kennedy and Johnson Administrations had averaged 11.0 interventions per year, there were only thirty-three in the eight years of Nixon and Ford, for an average of 4.1[32] In large measure, this reluctance to show force was due to the American popular reaction against Vietnam, which acted as a constraint on the ability of any administration to commit U.S. troops. But it also followed in part from the relaxation of the most extreme perceptions of the Soviet Union that followed inevitably from detente. Without a sharply negative view of an enemy, it is difficult to justify an activist foreign policy.

The Carter period: a new peak? (1977-1980)

The policymakers who had produced NSC-68 and the Gaither Report understood that if U.S.-Soviet detente continued, the positions for which they had fought would be undermined. The anti-Soviet forces, early in the 1970s, began to regroup. Winning allies from within the Nixon Administration (like James Schlesinger, who was forced out of his position as Defense Secretary in a highly publicized dispute with Kissinger), Paul Nitze, Eugene Rostow, Dean Rusk and other unreconstructed believers in the Soviet threat took steps to launch a new surge in anti-Soviet perceptions. While it is too early to tell whether their campaign will be as successful as the previous two, it is already clear that they are having considerable impact, particularly in the debate over the ratification of the second SALT treaty.

Veteran's Day, 1976, three days after the election, was the date on which the Committee on the Present Danger held a news conference to announce its perception of "a Soviet drive for dominance based upon an unparalleled military buildup."[33] Issuing a none-too-subtle warning to the recently elected Jimmy Carter, the Committee set itself up as the guardian of the national interest. From a position outside the new administration, it would lead the crusade for a resumption of cold war hostilities with the Soviet Union.

Behind the ideological fervor of the Committee was a host of statistics arguing that the Soviets had used the detente period to obtain military advantages (or near-advantages) over the United States. To support its case, the Committee—in opposition to Kissinger's doctrine—retreated to the traditional cold war view of Soviet intentions. For example, one of the leading

How to Organize a Cold War

NATIONAL STRATEGY INFORMATION CENTER, INC.
111 East 58th Street
New York, N.Y. 10022

Area Code 212—375-2912

May 24, 1976

Dr. Eugene V. Rostow
Professor of Law
Yale University
New Haven, CT 06520

Dear Gene:

Earnestly hoping for your acceptance, our Directors have author-
ized me to invite you to join our Board. (You should know that
we've been granted $1 million to "crank up" an all-out effort to
meet the current and growing threat from the USSR—whether in
military, ideological or economic warfare terms.)

You are fully aware, of course, that in terms of the shifting
military balance—and in our diplomatic credibility in much of the
world—the U.S. today is about where Britain was in 1938, with
the shadow of Hitler's Germany darkening all of Europe.

In this context, NSIC is opening a *full-scale Washington office* to:

intellectuals of the new offensive, Richard Pipes (a professor of
Russian history at Harvard), wrote an article in which he claimed
that the Russians were contemplating preparations for war with
the United States.[34]

In order to make the case for a Soviet threat to the United
States—especially in the post-detente context—the new cold
warriors followed the now established pattern of commissioning
a study group to report on the U.S.-Soviet military balance. For
years, the C.I.A. had been compiling estimates of the military
capabilities of other countries, including the Soviet Union.
Called national intelligence estimates (NIEs), these reports
became the official basis for strategic planning. Toward the end
of the Ford Administration, an official NIE came under scathing
criticism from some of the more extreme anti-Soviet policy

a) interact with policy echelons in the White House and Pentagon (where we still have many friends);
b) "tutor" Congressional Staffs, and brief members;
c) work with Trade Associations—with an interest in "defense"—which have Washington offices;
d) generate more public information through friends in the Washington press corps who write about military and foreign affairs.

I, personally, will move to Washington in September to supervise our "interface" operation. (We will also continue our "educational" program, which now reaches 350 universities.)

Please join with us!

With best regards, I am

Faithfully,
Frank R. Barnet

cc: Robert B .Burke
    Frank N. Trager

P.S.: Inasmuch as I'll be in Europe May 15-June 17 (attending NATO "think-tank" sessions in six Allied nations), if you have any questions, please feel free to contact Dr. Frank Trager, our Director of Studies.

I think you have in your files most of our Publications and our basic brochure; but, if there's anything else you need to refresh your understanding of our program, please let us know.

makers involved in the process. (One of them, retired General Daniel Graham, said that "there are more liberals per square foot in the CIA than in any other part of government.")[35] As a response to this criticism, President Ford in the spring of 1976 appointed a group of outsiders to review the NIEs. This study group, known as Team B, included men like Richard Pipes, Paul Nitze, and other members of what would become the Committee on the Present Danger. The Team B report was predictable. It argued that the previous NIEs had been wrong, that the Soviets were engineering a massive military build-up in order to pressure the West, and that a major U.S. response was needed. The Team B report was to the 1970s what the Gaither Report had been to the 1950s and NSC-68 to the 1940s.

Team B was only part of the picture of increasingly hostile

perceptions of Soviet intentions. Articles in *Commentary,* effective lobbying by the Pentagon and private think tanks, Republican Party assertiveness, and attempts to mobilize the cold war faction of the Democratic Party combined to produce a new wave of belligerency. But would the new wave turn into a peak? That depended on both the Russians and the policymakers within the Carter Administration.

Russian behavior was, as it always is, ambiguous. The Soviets had increased their spending on arms, although much of the new allocations went into defending the border with China. More importantly, the capacity of a country to operate effectively in the international system is part of its overall political and economic strength, and on that score, the Soviet Union was in its worst shape in years. It seemed to be facing an economic crisis, undermining its productive capacity. Its agricultural system was in such bad shape that it was dependent on the U.S. to feed its own population. Substantially in debt to the West, the Soviets were trying to compete in trade, without notable success. The overarching goal of Soviet foreign policy seemed to be a second arms limitation treaty with the U.S. Because of U.S. rapprochement with China, the Soviets were finally surrounded by hostile powers on all sides. One could argue, as some on the right did, that the Soviets might become more hostile precisely because they were weaker, but one could *not* argue that the Soviets were pursuing an unrelenting expansionist policy without doing considerable damage to the truth.

Within the Carter Administration, a major debate took place about how to evaluate the Soviet Union. Initially, Carter's response was to downplay the Soviet threat; he avoided the Committee on the Present Danger entirely when he named his foreign policy advisors, for example.[36] Then, when the right-wing campaign picked up, he tried to balance the views of Cyrus Vance, who took a "soft" position on the Russians, with those of Zbigniew Brzezinski, who was more of a confirmed cold warrior. Marshall Shulman, Carter's key Soviet advisor, said that the U.S. should seek both competition and cooperation with the Russians, which reflected the internal debates within the Administration but was irrelevant to the hurly-burly of domestic politics.[37] No clear-cut position on the nature of the Soviet threat seemed to emerge.

The confusion surrounding the Carter Administration's attitude toward the Soviet Union was expressed in Presidential Review Memorandum 10, a document that was meant to rival NSC-68 and the Gaither Report, but which achieved little

YALE UNIVERSITY
Law School
New Haven, Connecticut

Eugene V. Rostow

June 1, 1976

Mr. Frank R. Barnett
President
National Strategy Information Center, Inc.
111 East 58th Street
New York, New York 10022

Dear Frank,

I am honored to accept your invitation of May 24 to join the Board of the National Strategy Information Center. I am delighted that you are opening a Washington office to conduct a campaign of direct and large scale persuasion to Congress, the Executive Branch, Trade Associations and the press corps.

On the political and political-military side, as you know, our new Committee on the Present Danger, of which you will be an active member, is planning a comparable if more limited operation. It should be no problem to coordinate our activities, and indeed to act jointly on many issues.

I fully agree, as you know, with your estimate that we are living in a pre-war and not a post-war world, and that our posture today is comparable to that of Britain, France and the United States during the Thirties. Whether we are at the Rhineland or the Munich watershed remains to be seen. I won't quarrel with your dating!

I assume that you see the Strategic Review, which reprinted a speech I gave in New York last January. Do let me know if you do not have a copy.

Yours cordially,

[Gene]

cc: The Honorable David Packard
    The Honorable Henry H. Fowler
    The Honorable Paul Nitze
    Mr. Charles Tyroler
    Max M. Kampelman, Esq.
    The Honorable Charles Walker
    Professor C.B. Marshall
    Richard Allen, Esq.
    Mr. Lane Kirkland
    The Honorable James Schlesinger
    The Honorable Rita Hauser

because of its internal contradictions. PRM-10 has never been made public, but reports in the press indicate that it was composed of two parts.[38] One argued that between the two superpowers there existed "essential equivalence" in nuclear weapons, which meant that neither could effectively threaten the other by brandishing its strategic arms. However, a second portion concluded that conflict between the superpowers was still intense in certain key areas, especially the Middle East, where conventional arms were important. The gist of the report was that the U.S. should concentrate its efforts to gain superiority over the Soviet Union in Europe and the Middle East while trying to preserve the precarious balance in nuclear weapons that existed and would, in all likelihood, continue to exist. Written in this way, PRM-10 was acceptable to both the hardliners in the Carter camp like Samuel Huntington and Zbigniew Brzezinski and to the critics of cold war extremism like Paul Warnke and his aid, Lynn Davis. In this sense, PRM-10, like NSC-68, had as much to do with domestic political controversies as it did with the actual state of the world. Indeed, it was not as crucial to anti-Soviet perceptions as the Team B Report.

Until the issue of Russian troops in Cuba exploded, Carter's attempts to find a middle position had made the third peak of anti-Soviet hositility less severe than the previous ones. Through the SALT II talks, troop withdrawal negotiations in Europe, and refusals to intervene militarily in Iran and in Africa, the Carter Administration clearly resisted some of the most extreme cold war positions. But at the same time, Carter and his Defense Secretary Harold Brown, have also partially followed the anti-Soviet script. They have increased the defense budget, for example, much of it rationalized on an explicitly anti-Soviet basis. (Carter's State of the Union message calling for defense increases made numerous responses to the Truman era's Marshall Plan.)[39] And in public speeches at Annapolis and Wake Forrest, Carter sounded the anti-Soviet tocsin.[40] His response to the Russian troops in Cuba shows how tenuous his middle position was. A minor diplomatic issue has become a major political challenge to a weak president, and he has responded by turning it into a test of America's will and a demonstration of American power. Thus the third peak of anti-Soviet hostility was stunted at first, but it has grown and could become still worse.

From this review of the peaks and valleys of anti-Soviet sentiment since World War II, it becomes possible to make a few tentative conclusions.

First, while anti-communism is a more or less permanent

30

While anti-communism is a more or less permanent feature of American politics, anti-Soviet perceptions have gone through distinct phases.

feature of American politics, anti-Soviet perceptions have gone through distinct phases. Each increase in hostile perceptions has certain similarities. First, a group of officials or intellectuals—generally of a conservative persuasion—will make a strong case for adopting a more hostile interpretation of Soviet conduct over a more ambiguous one. Second, these generally right-wing views (although they are often associated with Democrats who take a "liberal" position on the domestic issues as well) create an atmosphere in which it becomes difficult for the incumbent president to ignore the increasingly hostile perception. Then, as a result of the new consensus, concrete acts—such as an increase in the defense budget or a foreign policy intervention—express the new hard-line position. The record shows that while the right-wing view of Soviet intentions never changes, what does change is the seriousness with which that view is taken within an incumbent administration.

Second, it begins to become clear that anti-Soviet perceptions reach a peak, not because certain policymakers intentionally engage in a campaign to redirect foreign policy (although some try to do this), but because various constellations of forces come together to give more negative perceptions of the Soviet threat greater credence. Political convenience rather than conspiracy produces a Soviet scare.

Third, a strong case can be made that the peaks of anti-Soviet hostility are not directly related to increases in the Soviet Union's "aggressiveness." To be sure, there is evidence of Soviet advances for each period of cold war hostility: Eastern Europe, especially Czeckoslovakia, for the first peak; Cuba for the second; and increased activity in Africa for the third. But it is difficult to discover a cause and effect. There has been a long history of conflict between the U.S. and the Soviet Union. *The real issue is not whether the Soviets become more aggressive, but whether the U.S. decides to view them as more aggressive* (and vice versa). For example, much evidence existed at each anti-Soviet peak to support an opposite interpretation of Soviet motives: postwar cooperation and signs from Stalin that he wanted to negotiate in the late 1940s; the change in the regime and decision to downplay military spending in the 1950s, combined with Soviet willingness to negotiate a test-ban treaty; and deliberate Soviet restraint in Vietnam, Iran, and other countries, combined with an overwhelming desire to conclude a SALT II treaty in the 1970s. U.S.-Soviet accommodation over the postwar period is fully as impressive as the antagonism between them. *What needs to be explained then is why, when the evidence is always ambiguous, the more negative perceptions develop at the time they do.* Specific Soviet actions have something to do with the answer, but we must look elsewhere for a full explanation.

Finally, if actions by the Soviet Union are of only tangential importance in understanding the rise and fall of the Soviet threat, then political events at home may well be more crucial. The question becomes whether it is possible to discover similarities in the three periods when anti-Soviet perceptions peaked and began to influence policy. If there are common features to all these periods, then one can conclude that domestic politics may be more important in explaining the Soviet threat than relations between the United States and the Soviet Union.

In the next five chapters, I will examine five domestic features that each of the peaks has, to one degree or another, in common. These include: the pattern of party politics; cycles of presidential strength and weakness; inter-service rivalries; debates over the locus of foreign policy; and patterns of economic growth.

Chapter III:
The Center Cannot Hold

The most striking feature that all three peaks of anti-Soviet hostility have in common is that on each occasion, the Democrats held the presidency. Does this mean, as Senator Robert Dole charged during the 1976 election campaign, that the Democrats are a war party? It does, but only because the Republicans force them to be. In order to understand the role that domestic politics play in raising the level of intensity of the Soviet threat, it is important to examine the way the two political parties treat foreign policy.

My argument in this chapter will be that hostile perceptions of the Soviet Union tend to occur under similar political conditions. First, a new president, generally a Democrat, assumes office. During this time, the right wing organizes itself around the notion of a Soviet threat, a politically safe issue for them since they are out of power and need not concern themselves with putting new policies into effect. Pressure from the right makes the newly installed president vulnerable. If there was equally strong pressure from the left, in favor of programs oriented toward greater equality and a foreign policy permitting smaller defense budgets, the new president would not be forced to lean rightwards. But without a strong left, Democratic presidents invariably adopt a more aggressive foreign policy as a way of protecting their political base. This also gives them the appearance of being bold and decisive, which cuts down some of the need to adopt aggressive domestic programs—ones that would antagonize big business and conservative interest groups. For all these reasons, the structure of domestic political alignments and coalitions comes to have as much to do with an increase in hostile perceptions of Soviet power as any actions taken by the Soviet Union.

At the end of World War II there was a deep uncertainty about the form that American politics would take. The New Deal coalition of Franklin Roosevelt was no longer in an unchallenged position as conservative ideas became more popular. Starting late in the 1930s and then continuing through the war, business had fought strenuously to regain respectability in America. White Southerners, who had been part of a populist tradition at one point in time, were turning conservative in the face of the race issue. Isolationism, an important current in American political life with both Socialist and Republican roots, had lodged itself in the latter party as the former ceased to exist.

When he became president, Harry Truman was fully aware of the resurging conservative sentiment in the country. Without the personal magnetism that had enabled Roosevelt to survive, Truman had to make important political decisions, and he had very little time in which to do so. Most importantly, he had two options as he faced the right-wing thrust. He could, on the one hand, make an attempt to unify the New Deal coalition and face the right head-on. Such an approach meant moving to the left by mobilizing new constituents among the working class, minorities and women and fighting for new policies like medical insurance, housing, and extensions of social welfare. Alternatively, he could attempt to meet the right's challenge by co-opting it, moving in a conservative direction by restricting new constituencies and not being aggressive about new policies.

Either course meant risks for Truman. If he moved to the right, he risked disaffection from liberals. Business, the white South, and isolationists would not support a Democratic president without demanding a price, and in order to win their allegiance Truman would have to promise incentives to business, concessions to racism, and appeals to American nativism, none of which would please the inheritors of Roosevelt's progressivism. Yet if Truman moved to the left, he would allow the demagogues that were rising throughout the land to smear him with being soft on everything. No wonder that Truman tried his hardest to avoid a choice. He searched desperately for a position in the center, one that would forestall the extremes from both directions and enable him to build a new political coalition. In this he was successful, for in the postwar period a new centrist political coalition did come to power, one that has dominated the Democratic Party—and therefore America—for a generation. This coalition can be called "Cold War liberalism," for it combined a New Deal attachment to the welfare state with strong support for a cold war foreign policy.[41] The cold war liberal coalition included business, labor, intellectuals, and the military. The building of this remarkable cold war liberal coalition could never have been achieved without one essential ingredient: the fear of the Soviet threat.

Anti-communism was capable of working like magic in containing both the right and the left versions of how to organize America. Business, for example, had traditionally opposed using government as a stimulant for the economy. Rejecting Keynesian economics as subversive, most American businessmen—with the exception of far-sighted groups like the Committee on Economic

34

Development—felt that increased government activity would mean higher budgets and higher taxes. For the economic activists around Truman, this opposition presented a dilemma: how could they involve the state in macroeconomic management without antagonizing business sentiment? High defense budgets solved the problem: they would be used to stimulate the economy without invoking opposition from the right. While Truman personally remained unconvinced—he called for limits on the defense budget and, even when he approved increases, he demanded that they be "stretched out"[42]—the political logic of the situation overwhelmed the president. Before Truman's presidency was over, the defense budget had become an economic stimulant. And when the new money was spent in the South and West, it also brought Southerners and former isolationists into the coalition. In this manner, the military budget ultimately became the unifying force that prevented the right from setting itself up in successful opposition to the new centrist consensus.

At the same time, anti-communism did not necessarily have to alienate the left. True, the Marshall Plan and the foreign policy of containment would mean that a small segment of the left—the one that united around Henry Wallace and the Progressive Party—would venture out on its own. But by adopting progressive issues like housing and health care (even while restructuring them in ways that could win some business support), Truman was able to preserve his symbolic links to the New Deal and to minimize his losses. Meanwhile, other segments of the left would support him fully in his newly discovered anti-communism. Those liberals who had fought against the Communist Party (and often lost) could ride the wave of anti-communism and obtain their revenge. Union leaders like Walter Reuther, ambitious politicians like Hubert Humphrey and Paul Douglas, intellectuals in the Americans for Democratic Action—all were as strongly anti-communist as the Republicans.[43] They could be counted on to be enthusiasts for the centrist course and to mobilize the voters and write the platforms that would sustain it. But, once again, there could be no successful attempt to win this segment of the liberal community—and to isolate the more radical Communist Party and its sympathizers—without making some strong claims about the danger that Russia posed.

Besides this magical political quality of the Soviet threat, broad agreement in the center of the political spectrum gave U.S. foreign policy an apolitical quality, as if it had nothing to do with partisan strife but was a unified response to an external enemy. For most of the postwar period, American foreign policy had

In a few short years, debates over the direction of American foreign policy abruptly stopped. Neither the isolationist right nor the progressive peace lobby could win a hearing for its point of view as the cold war liberal coalition came to dominate the political spectrum.

been described as bipartisan, a process that began in the late 1940s when President Truman won support for his initiatives from Senator Arthur Vandenberg. Because Vandenberg was a Republican and a conservative, his support for Truman undercut the potentially powerful right-wing opposition to an active foreign policy. Foreign policy was therefore thought to be "above" partisan strife.

Yet bipartisanship from the start was inherently partisan. Although liberal Democrats may have prided themselves on how cleverly they co-opted the right, in actuality they paid a high price, for they were forced to become more conservative and bellicose in order to keep the right's support. In effect, it meant that if the Democrats adopted the Republican's hyperbole, the Republicans would charitably restrain their criticism. Thus was a certain pattern established. First, a conservative Republican would wonder aloud whether the U.S. was doing all it could to remain the number one military power in the world. Then a Democratic president would assure the nation that, yes, we were as strong as we could be. Having approved a few new weapons systems, sponsored an increase in the defense budget, and intervened somewhere around the world, the Democrat would obtain assurance from the conservative critic that, yes indeed, we seemed to be on the right track. In this matter, bipartisanship insured that debates over national security policy would always be skewed sharply to the right. (Yet, it seems, not sharply enough: in 1979, the Republicans officially repudiated bipartisanship, to enable them to criticize the Carter Administration even more harshly than they did Truman, Kennedy, or Johnson.)

Given all these currents, it is no wonder that the Soviet threat became such an important feature of American politics after World War II. International political events clearly were an aspect of cold war hostility, but one simply cannot ignore the internal dynamics of U.S. party politics in trying to understand why the more negative perceptions of the Soviet Union were accepted over alternative images. Moreover, American party politics continued to influence domestic perceptions of the Soviet threat. In a few short years, debates over the direction of American foreign policy abruptly stopped. Neither the isolationist right nor the progressive peace lobby could win a hearing for its point of view as the cold war liberal coalition came to dominate the political spectrum.

Secure in its hegemony, cold war liberalism was the lifeblood of the Democratic Party in the postwar period. In consequence, all postwar Democratic presidents have found themselves in the position of being forced to adopt negative perceptions of Soviet conduct. John F. Kennedy, for example, faced a potential stalemate similar to Truman's. Barely elected, and with the conservative bloc strong in Congress, Kennedy had little room for political maneuver. Substantial segments of his own party distrusted him, either because they viewed him as an illegitimate heir to Adlai Stevenson or because they were suspicious of his urbane cosmopolitanism. The Republicans saw in his election an opportunity to increase the belligerency that had become central to their role in the bipartisan process. In short, for all his talk about activism and idealism, Kennedy's hold on political power was precarious.

Kennedy and his advisors were convinced that the public was far to the right of themselves, and therefore they were wary of doing too much. But at the same time, Democrats claim that the Republicans are the "do nothing" party, and in order to distinguish themselves from stand-pattism, they have to do something once in power. Torn between the need to do something and the fear of doing anything, Kennedy was left with the traditional course of waging full scale battles against universally recognized enemies. Primary among these was the Soviet Union. From the moment of his Inaugural—when he called for increases in air power, the building of nuclear missiles, and the development of the Polaris submarine—to the end of his presidency, Kennedy sought to expand the military budget. And his advisors searched the world to find a place where the new military might could be demonstrated. For Kennedy, the answer to his domestic political dilemma was to be aggressive around the world, and thus to rekindle the fear of the Soviet threat.

In retrospect, there was an air of inevitability to the resurgence of negative images of the Soviet threat in the early years of the Kennedy Administration. If, in a democratic society, domestic pressures shape foreign policy responses, then the only direction in which the Administration could move was to the right. By 1960, whatever remained of the left had disintegrated. First, the anti-communism of the Truman period and then McCarthyism had wiped out radicalism as an effective force in American life. Then the Eisenhower years had worshipped a benumbing apathy that left little place for controversy and dissent. While the seeds of the civil rights movement were planted in the late 1950s, no significant opposition to the assumption of a global foreign policy on the part of the United States was able to make itself felt. Without anything to fear on the left, Kennedy had to worry only about the right. His belligerency toward the Russians protected that flank. Thus, so long as he kept alive the Soviet threat, Kennedy had a relatively clear field to himself. An aggressive foreign policy therefore became a crucial link in his governing coalition.

Lyndon Johnson, who inherited so much from Kennedy inherited the mantle of cold war liberalism as well; indeed Johnson became the single most conspicuous example of the tendency to fight external enemies and internal social problems at the same time. Johnson, unlike Kennedy, pushed for and obtained a pathbreaking legislative program. In so doing, he destroyed one of the central myths of American politics, that the country is so conservative it would never support changes in its political practices. On the contrary, Johnson's efforts showed that with an aggressive platform and with a favorable legislative majority, movements in a leftward direction were feasible. Yet having stretched the realm of the possible in domestic life, Johnson narrowed it in foreign policy. Rather than drawing the conclusion that the right was a paper tiger, he fell into the traditional Democratic fear of a rightwing backlash. Certain that his Great Society left him exposed to the Neanderthals, Johnson did everything in his power to prove how aggressive he could be overseas, first sponsoring the invasion of the Dominican Republic and then ruining his own accomplishments by persevering in Vietnam. Had Johnson carried over into foreign policy the lessons of the Great Society, he would have broken the cold war liberal pattern, liberated the Democratic Party from its need to exaggerate the Soviet threat, and conceivably have become one of the greatest of American presidents. Instead he was forced to retire in disgrace.

If the peaks of anti-Soviet hostility have certain political features in common, so should the valleys. And indeed, just as the former are dominated by Democrats pursuing cold war liberal policies, the latter are dominated by Republicans with a different domestic political agenda. The Republican Party, at the presidential level, does not have to face the same kind of domestic dilemmas that bedevil liberal Democrats. Eisenhower, fo example, simply was not as vulnerable to the right. It is true that the right, in the form of Senator Joseph McCarthy and his allies, did try to attack the General, but the notion that such a conservative man as Eisenhower could be "soft" on communism was so ludicrous that this tactical mistake began McCarthy's downfall. Nor did Eisenhower face any pressure from the left. The debates between activist idealists and realistic powerbrokers on the left had been won so handily by the latter that all the Democrats could do was to accuse Eisenhower of not being anti-communist *enough.* Immune to the need to build a domestic governing coalition, Eisenhower therefore had no particular interest in choosing the most hostile possible interpretations of Soviet conduct. Such domestic freedom gave Eisenhower's foreign policy enormous potential room to maneuver, although the president chose not to exercise his potential very much. A genuinely conservative administration did not need the image of a hostile Soviet threat in the same way that a would-be conservative one did.

Nixon and Kissinger were in a similarly favorable position. Nixon hoped to fashion an "emerging Republican majority" by uniting the white working class of the North with conservatives in the South and West over a strategy of trying to roll back the social gains experienced by minorities during the 1960s.[44] To accomplish this task, Nixon did need foreign policy bellicosity, but he could rely on largely symbolic anti-communism for domestic consumption while searching for big-power accommodations with the Soviet Union. Highly symbolic foreign policy militancy works better for Republicans than for Democrats, for the latter's vulnerability to the right means that they often have to combine actions with words. The former, because they are the right, find that words suffice to shore up their domestic image of "toughness." So long as he reduced U.S. troop levels in Vietnam, Nixon was free to do most of what he wanted in foreign policy. It was not detente that disgraced him, but his own domestic arrogance.

Thus, by 1976 we can see a clear pattern emerge, in which the shape of domestic political coalitions clearly has an impact in determining whether an administration will choose a highly negative image of Soviet conduct, leading to confrontation, or a big power view, leading to some form of accommodation. One of the most crucial political issues on the current agenda is whether this pattern must continue in the near future. The message from the experience of the Carter Administration is mixed.

Jimmy Carter, like Kennedy, assumed power after eight years

> **Carter's decision to tolerate, and even encourage, his own cold warriors gave him short-term breathing space at the expense of long-term impotence.**

of Republican rule. Moreover, his predecessor, like Kennedy's, had taken actions that reduced the level of tension in the world, however shortsighted he might have been in other areas. Under Nixon and Kissinger the most negative images of the Soviet Union had receeded substantially. By relaxing the cold war, Nixon performed an invaluable service for Carter. He did what no Democrat could ever do, which was to prepare the groundwork for some reasonable order in the world. As a result of Nixon's and Kissinger's endorsement of detente and because of their support for a strategic arms limitation treaty with the Russians, the anti-Soviet cold warriors were isolated for the first time in the postwar period. In this way, Nixon put Jimmy Carter in the position of being the first postwar Democrat that did not *need* the cold war. Whenever the hawks began their attack, which they were certain to do, Carter had a sure-fire response: he could claim that he was merely following the principles of his impeccably anti-communist predecessor. Carter, had he been a more astute politician, might have used bipartisanship to protect himself from the cold warriors in the rightwing of his party, just as "moderate" Republicans had used the concept in the late 1940s to protect themselves from the extreme right of their party.

The verdict on the Carter Administration will not be in for awhile, but it seems safe to suggest that Carter's refusal to walk through the opening that Nixon provided him will turn out to be one of the major political blunders of recent times. By the time that Carter had assumed office, the length and intensity of the cold war had transformed many key features of American politics. Although Truman's support of cold war policies had associated with it opportunistic aspects, by the late 1970s many Democrats had come to accept the Soviet threat as an indispensible part of their outlook on the world. Defense plants, hawkish labor unions, support for Israel, and macroeconomic stimulation had all combined with the power of military men, contractors, and spies to produce a firm coalition in favor of increased defense spending and a renewed foreign policy militancy. Senators like Henry Jackson and Daniel Patrick Moynihan, former policy makers like Paul Nitze and his friends in the Committee on the Present Danger, and columnists like Joseph Kraft were leading the chorus in favor of a cold war coda. What did it matter if these men had a distorted view of the world and that Carter knew it? They seemed to be a political problem, and to the president, that was all that mattered.

Carter's decision to tolerate, and even encourage, his own cold warriors gave him short-term breathing space at the expense of long-term impotence. By moving in their direction, he bought security from the rightwing of his party, but also undermined his ability to forge a broad domestic coalition because he would be unable either to fight inflation successfully or to support new welfare programs. (Cold war defense budgets are so inflationary that they destroy simultaneous attempts to keep prices down in other areas, and they are so expensive that they make it impossible to have both guns and butter.) Moreover, Carter's tolerance of the cold war critics on his right—his seeming eagerness to win their support by yielding to them on new weapons like the M-X missile, for example—actually undermines his genuine foreign policy initiatives by giving the cold war view of the world more credence than it would otherwise have.

Emboldened by Carter's failure to stand up for his earlier principles, the right knows that it can criticize as much as it chooses. Carter has not seen that concessions to the cold warriors make them stronger, not weaker. Had he been more direct about his reforms, he would not, in all likelihood, be facing a Congress that repudiates his Africa policy and undermines all his attempts to negotiate even very conservative treaties. And so, instead of having used Nixon's softening of the cold war to increase his options domestically, Carter finds himself unable to commit the United States to policies that are fresh and more in accord with the economic conditions of the day. (Cold war liberalism was predicated on large budgets, which implies an expanding economy; the notion is not economically feasible in periods of stagnation. For more on this point, see Chapter VII below.) Thus Carter plays cold war liberal politics even as the conditions which allow for cold war liberal politics disappear. This is why the right's opposition to SALT and detente seem so strong, even though the Carter Administration has—in Africa, around SALT, and in terms of some new weapons like the B-1 bomber— tried to fashion non-cold war solutions.

There will be those who will insist until their last breath that the reason why the fear of the Soviet Union becomes stronger in the United States is because of aggressive actions taken by the Russians. The increase in cold war sentiment after 1976, they will argue, has nothing to do with Democrats and Republicans but is solely due to the fact that the Soviets are rapidly expanding their military capabilities and taking advantage of perceived American weakness by becoming more adventuresome in Africa and the Middle East. To be sure, the global power situation has changed in recent years. In particular, all the advanced nations of the world have lost power, including the United States, as Third World revolutions and the rise of China to world power status have altered the nature of international relations. The U.S. without question is no longer the unchallenged hegemonic power it once was. But this alone cannot explain the rise of anti-Soviet perceptions and the militant opposition to the SALT II treaty in the U.S. Senate. It is equally as plausible that the decline in power of the U.S. would lead to greater (implicit) accommodation with the Russians, for both countries are losing power simultaneously. One factor which explains why the specific response to the general problem of declining power should be a possible new peak in anti-Soviet perceptions is the domestic political balance. Once Carter opted for "cold war liberal politics as usual" as the alternative to finding a progressive governing strategy that would win the loyalty of blacks, unions, women and other such groups, then inevitably a pattern of high defense budgets, fears of a Soviet military buildup, and opposition to detente and SALT would be given prominent place in domestic debate.

From this review of the political features that the cycles of anti-Soviet belligerency have in common, it is possible to offer some thoughts on the conditions under which policymakers in America will adopt a more negative perception of Russian intentions.

1. The Soviet threat will nearly always be more exaggerated under Democratic presidents than under Republican ones. Many Democrats are firm cold warriors.

2. This does not mean, however, that the Democrats are to be blamed for the cold war and the Republicans absolved. The former party becomes more belligerent only when it is egged on by the latter. Republicans concentrate, when out of power, on American weakness, for they have a domestic program that has never been very popular. Even though their ideas are often more symbolic than real, the Democrats take them seriously, more seriously sometimes than they take themselves, and constantly try to implement some of their notions.

3. The main reason why the Soviet threat will not go away, even when conditions demand that it should, is because of the absence of a strong left in the United States. Without a left, Democratic presidents have little choice but to turn to the right in

foreign policy.

4. Three features of the American political system—Republican opportunism, Democratic control over the policy-making process, and the lack of a left—combined to intensify expressions of the Soviet threat. If any of these factors are missing—if the Republicans were to come to power, if a left were to come into existence, or if the Democrats were to become the loyal opposition—then the Soviet threat would be downplayed. But when all three conditions are present, then American politics tends to exaggerate negative perceptions of Soviet conduct. As Jimmy Carter discovered, he had two choices: he could have tried to lead the development of a more peaceful public opinion in the United States or he would be forced to concede enormous ground to the anti-Soviet cold war critics. Too cautious to do the former, he has had to rely on the latter. And once again the Soviet threat has been rekindled, not because the Soviet Union has done anything differently than what it usually does, but because the domestic political constellation in the United States forced the issue to once again take its central place in the political firmament.

Chapter IV:
The Presidency
and Its Enemies

After Vietnam and Watergate, many observers think of a strong presidency as being responsible for some of the abuses in the American political system. Yet there is a peculiar way in which the peaks of anti-Soviet hostility correspond, not so much to the strength of the presidency, but to its weakness. In this chapter, I will set forward the proposition that high points of anti-Soviet perception correspond with attempts by presidents to defend the power of the office against attacks upon it.

Much of American ideology is sympathetic to weak government, but the American economic system since the latter part of the nineteenth century has demanded a strong one. Traditionally, therefore, there have been cycles in which activist presidents have expanded the power of the presidency, only to see its power watered down in later years. In the period since World War II, there have been a number of occasions when power seemed to be passing away from the presidency, commencing a cycle of weak executive power. It has been precisely during those periods when negative perceptions of an external enemy heightened, and one consequence was to preserve presidential power.

Over the long historical sweep of American life, the fear of centralized political power has never gone away.[45] So long as America was a rural society, its anti-government bias did not interfere with the serious business of living one's life as best as one could. But the growth of a national economy required expanded national governance, and eventually that expanded governmental activity encouraged the growth of the executive branch, the only branch capable of coordinating it. When the Great Depression hit America, the need for a strong state increased, and it increased even further as foreign and military policies assumed a position of unchallenged prominence in American life.[46] A national longing for small and simple government was in conflict with a national and international need for a powerful and centralized executive branch.

The result was a deep contradiction at the heart of American political life. On the one hand, the specific political and economic features of a modern political economy—giant corporations, an expanded state that served their needs with giant public construction projects, a welfare state, and a global foreign policy

44

aimed at stabilizing the world's markets—all demanded an active, strong executive. On the other hand, popular ideology, the Constitution, local elites, and competitive sector businessmen all preferred a weak central government and a passive executive. There was no way to reconcile these two demands. As a result, American politics has been characterized by a cyclical pattern in which activist presidents like Theodore Roosevelt and Woodrow Wilson strengthened the executive but were immediately followed by others who relaxed presidential power and passed it back to the states. Until World War II, every single increase in presidential power brought forth a decrease later on.

When Franklin Roosevelt died and was replaced by Truman, a reaction against presidential power set in. From the states, from Congress, and from the heartlands of America came demands to simplify life, to return power to the people, and to reestablish normality. For example, Truman's globally oriented advisors were telling him how important it was to retain some U.S. troops in Europe in order to maximize American leverage there after the war ended. But so strong was the demand for a more normal existence that Truman was effectively prevented from so doing; the troops came home. This experience with demobilization made it clear to presidential activists (like Clark Clifford) that unless steps were taken to curb such sentiment, all the gains that had been made by the executive since 1932 might be lost. Without a strong executive, men like Clifford reasoned, the U.S. would be unable to exercise world leadership; its role in the world's markets would be undermined by foreign competition; its welfare state would be in danger; and the entire political coalition that had brought the U.S. out of the depression and had fought the war would fall apart.

Republican electoral victories, first in 1946 and then in 1948, had made the Congress, particularly the Senate, the locus of the cyclical attack on presidential power. The old-fashioned American right-wing Republicans were arguing that a global foreign policy was a cover-up for presidential dictatorship, a device for insuring the domination of the economy by internationally-oriented, monopolistic American firms. As the right wing became stronger, Truman's ability to preserve a strong presidency became weaker.

The rise of a negative perception of Soviet conduct must be seen in the light of these debates over presidential power. This is not to argue that policymakers deliberately exaggerated the Soviet threat in order to keep the executive strong, although there is evidence that on two occasions, to be discussed momentarily, such specific intentions were present. But it is to suggest that the entire atmosphere associated with the fears of an external enemy is conducive to making the argument for strong presidential power seem more valid.[47]

One case of a fairly deliberate decision by the Truman Administration to adopt a negative perception on Soviet conduct in order to protect the presidency came over the Truman Doctrine. Truman's advisors had convinced the president that securing public support for aid to Greece and Turkey demanded an "all out" speech portraying Soviet activities as a major threat to the security of the United States. To do so would be to ignore evidence that events in both countries were local in scope, the result of long historical forces, and not a result of Soviet "aggression." Two of the most prominent Soviet specialists in the United States, George Kennan and Charles Bohlen, both strongly anti-communist, blanched when they saw a draft of Truman's speech because of its provocative overtones. Their objections were overruled on the grounds that in order to win Senate approval of a new foreign policy (the Senate was attracted to isolationism and was wary of giving up its role in foreign policy, as an aggressive new doctrine like containment would force it to do), a militant anti-Soviet speech was essential.[48] Thus cold war perceptions were cultivated, not because of international affairs, but because of domestic political conditions.

A more extreme example of the deliberate cultivation of anti-Soviet perceptions in order to protect the executive branch against its enemies came over Berlin, the hottest seat in the cold war. In 1948 the U.S. was shocked when a cable arrived from General Lucius Clay, commander of American forces in West Germany, painting Soviet aggression in such strong terms that men like Kennan felt a war to be in the offing. Later, after the damage had been done in terms of both solidifying American distrust of the Soviet role in Germany and confirming the Russian view of American aggressive tendencies, Clay admitted that he had sent his cable for domestic political reasons in the U.S. "It's primary purpose," wrote the General's biographer, "was to assist the military chiefs in their Congressional testimony; it was not, in Clay's opinion, related to any change in Soviet strategy."[49] American policymakers were apparently willing to risk war in order to prevent Congress from reasserting its power over the decision making process. In such ways, the downswing of the cycle away from executive power that would have "naturally" occurred was prevented, and under Truman the executive was able to hold onto its prerogatives in the face of a general distrust of the executive branch.

Yet these are extreme examples, not representative of general

46

Both Kennedy and Johnson found themselves comfortable with a foreign policy stance that was activist and, because it was activist, maintained the necessity of strong presidential power.

---

trends. In most cases, the relationship between negative perceptions of the Soviet Union and decisions to preserve presidential power are more the result of a coincidence of interest than they are directly intentional. It tends to be the case that those presidents who are most in need of an active foreign policy in order to hold together their governing coalition (see Chapter III) are those presidents who accept as essential the need for a strong presidency as a solution to domestic and foreign needs.

John Kennedy, for example, began his campaign for the presidency convinced that Eisenhower had done the U.S. a great disservice by not being a sufficiently aggressive executive. In early 1960s, Kennedy rejected a "restricted concept of the Presidency," and said that the nation's leader should become "the vital center of action in our whole scheme of government." Moreover, Kennedy seemed to endorse unconstitutional actions, at least to those conservatives that take a restricted reading of the Constitution, when he said that the president should be "prepared to exercise the fullest powers of his office—all that are specified and some that are not."[50] At the time, these seemed like progressive sentiments. To some degree they were, for Kennedy (at some point down the road) wanted to extend those trends that broadened the welfare state and protected civil liberties. But, as would soon become clear, his notion of an expanded presidency also meant unchecked foreign interventions and the cultivation of a sense of permanent crisis.

Kennedy practiced what he preached. During his administration, tendencies toward concentrated power increased. Distrustful of the State Department, Kennedy placed responsibility for foreign affairs in the hands of a few men on his personal staff. Those men generally showed contempt for Congress' role in foreign policy, reaching a high point when Nicholas Katzenbach, a Kennedy aide who stayed on to work for Lyndon Johnson, told Congress that it could just go ahead and impeach the president if it did not like what he was doing. This distrust of all agencies of power outside the presidency was characteristic of both the Kennedy and the Johnson Administrations. For them, highly

47

dramatic foreign policy crises, requiring decisive presidential action, added to the glamor of their administrations, and also worked to still any thoughts that Congress, local elites, conservative defenders of the Constitution, or ordinary people might have about a simpler political system in which the president did not have such awesome power. Both Kennedy and Johnson found themselves comfortable with a foreign policy stance that was activist and, because it was activist, maintained the necessity of strong presidential power.

No president undermined the power of the executive more than did Richard Nixon through his clumsy attempts to expand it. Although a strong executive had in the past been favored by Democrats and opposed by Republicans, Nixon confounded the pattern by expanding presidential power in order to pursue conservative goals. It was a master stroke. Liberals detested the ends but admired the means; conservatives were enraptured by the ends but distrusted the means. Neither side, therefore, was in a position to criticize Nixon for what he was doing. Had Nixon successfully carried out his conservative coup d'etat, he would have realigned American attitudes toward the question of presidential power.[51]

The Watergate scandal was thus both a boom and a bust to the believers in an active presidency that congregated around the Democratic Party. It disgraced Nixon and opened the way for the Democrats to reoccupy the White House. But at the same time, Nixon had given a bad name to presidential power, and a strong executive was still central to the practice of the Democratic Party, since advanced capitalism, the welfare state, and global ambitions were still very much on its mind. At the height of Watergate prominent Democrats were trying desperately to make a distinction between executive power—which was good, and Nixon's power—which was bad. Joseph Califano, who would become Jimmy Carter's Secretary of Health, Education, and Welfare, insisted that "a strong presidency is essential to the future of this nation and the freedom of our people" and implied that Nixon had failed not because he had too much power, but because he had too little.[52] The biggest challenge facing the Carter Administration was how to restore the legitimate authority of a strong presidency after both Vietnam and Watergate had reawakened the traditional American desire to fracture political power and keep it weak.

Carter has not been all that successful at this task. Despite his best efforts to transform the energy crisis into the "moral equivalent of war," skepticism of emergencies has been too firmly ingrained in the American people at this point to produce much

48

of a response. Even though Carter's former Energy Secretary James Schlesinger rants and raves about the need for sacrifice in the face of external challenges—much as he did when he was Nixon's Secretary of Defense and the threat was from the Communists, not the Arabs—there seems to be no great willingness on the part of the American people to disturb their comforts for the sake of a crisis in which they do not believe. What the energy experience shows is that in this case the American people will not accept the kinds of conditions that lead the president to expand his powers.

The preference for normality that characterizes the American mood in the late 1970s disrupts the relationship between attempts to maintain a strong president and negative perceptions of an external enemy, though most of the ingredients for the resurgence of anti-Soviet hostility are present. The chief national security advisor, Zbigniew Brzezinksi, is a confirmed cold warrior who has tried his hardest to develop a traditional cold war liberal foreign policy. At one point, it was rumored, he almost convinced Carter to intervene in Africa in order to put a stop to Soviet influence on that continent. And Carter has responded to such proddings by occasionally making hair-raising speeches aimed at the Soviet Union, as he did at Wake Forrest College in 1978. He has also invoked 1940s-type language in talking about the threat to Europe in order to justify his decision to seek defense budget increases, as if the Russians are poised and ready to pounce on Western Europe at the first sign of American weakness. Yet there is something half-hearted about these incantations, as if Carter is merely going through a ritual in raising the Soviet threat. Compared to the fervid language of earlier periods, the Russian menace is invoked in an obligatory fashion, almost apologetically, as if policymakers have no other language for speaking about the world. If the domestic atmosphere permitted the executive greater leeway to expand his power, it would probably follow that the Soviet threat would be asserted with more convincing vigor. The Administration is going slow on both counts. It will be some time before any president can have all the power that existed before Nixon, and for that reason, it will also be some time before the Soviet threat can be revivified in the true-believer fashion of a more naive earlier time.

Unless one wishes to claim that the relationship between the attacks on presidential power and the cultivation of the Soviet threat is purely coincidental, the following relationships seem worth pondering:

A Carter Advisor Speaks on Presidential Power

. . . it is essential that there be more effective centralized control over East-West economic relations within the executive branch of government. This is necessary so that the various decisions that have to be made concerning trade, technological transfers, scientific contacts, credits, and grain exports will be brought together at a single point and effectively related to the foreign policy purposes that the United States is pursuing at any given time. This can only be done adequately through the framework of the National Security Council (NSC) . . .

The central need is to provide the president with the means to engage in creative and flexible economic diplomacy with the Soviets. There has been much discussion recently about untying the president's hands in foreign policy . . . It is equally important to untie the president's hands so that the United States can capitalize on its economic resources in its relations with the Soviets . . .

It is fairly clear that the nature of the Soviet political system prevents the Soviets from correcting their economic deficiencies. It would be truly ironic, even tragic, if it should turn out that the nature of the American political system prevents this nation from capitalizing on its very real economic advantages. That need not be the case.

Samuel P. Huntington, then coordinator of national security planning at the National Security Council, speaking at West Point, June, 1978.

Huntington, who gained enormous notoriety when he wrote a report for the Trilateral Commission arguing that America had become too democratic, here urges centralization of policy in a manner that has become almost reflexive for believers in strong presidential action.

1. An important reason for the cycle of anti-Soviet perception may lie in the fact that strong executive leadership is necessary to govern an advanced capitalist society with a global foreign policy, while ideology, tradition, and culture in America all conspire against the permanent existence of a strong presidency.

In this sense, one factor associated with the frequency of the Soviet threat is the weakness of the executive branch, for if its power were more secure, it would not need to exaggerate external measures in order to hold on to the power that it had accumulated. Truman, Kennedy and Carter were all in precarious political positions when the Soviet threat increased.

2. Negative perceptions of Soviet intentions are likely to arise at times when a weak but activist-oriented president has just been elected. If the new president faces a "natural" cycle in which power is due to pass away from the presidency, he will find that anti-Soviet feelings generate an atmosphere which preserves presidential power. Similarly, if a president comes to power after his predecessor has in some way discredited a strong presidency, there will be substantial pressure to develop a negative interpretation of the motives of an external enemy.

3. Thus, domestic political struggles over the nature of the presidency have some relationship to, even if they do not necessarily directly cause, peaks in the perception of anti-Soviet hostility. A study by the Brookings Institution, for example, found that the number of foreign adventures rose as the popularity of the president went up.[53] The best method of generating broad support in a pluralistic and highly fractured political system seems to be through foreign policy actions.

Chapter V:
The Politics of
Inter-Service Rivalry

The modern Executive is not only one branch of government among many, but a system of government unto itself containing numerous branches within it. As the presidency has become more vital to the governing of modern economy with a global foreign policy, the most important political conflicts begin to take place, not over it, but within it. For example, disputes between the CIA and the National Security Council often become bitter, as do arguments between the NSC and the Department of State. Those debates in turn lead to changes in American foreign policy.

Even within single branches of the executive, disputes over "turf" are likely to be serious. In this chapter, I will argue that the most important of these disputes—arguments between the military services for a greater share of the defense dollar—are directly related to the peaks of anti-Soviet perception. My point will be that the most negative perceptions of an external enemy tend to occur when the military services cannot agree on their proper share of the budget and make their differences public, whereas the valleys in anti-Soviet perception occur at times of relative peace between the three service branches.

In an age of nuclear weapons and multifaceted wars, the distinction between an army (land), a navy (sea), and an air force (air) makes less sense than it ever did, militarily speaking. From a strictly geo-political point of view, the nature of modern war demands an integrated fighting unit, one that can combine land, air, and sea operations. But however much sense integration makes militarily, there are substantial obstacles to such unification. Each military service is a bureaucratic empire, jealously guarding its self-interest by exaggerating what it does best and denigrating the capabilities of its opponents. Each, moreover, has its own constituency—contractors, legislators, supportive interest groups and ideologues—that it can mobilize at a moment's notice when it feels that it is about to be short-changed. Sometimes the wars fought between the service branches seem to rival the wars fought overseas in their intensity.

Since the end of World War II there have been repeated attempts to establish or to disestablish the equilibrium in power between the services. Such attempts generally occur in one of two ways. First, one branch, convinced that it has gained power over the others, attempts to sponsor a "reorganization" that will solidify into bureaucratic permanence its hegemony. Alternatively, another branch, feeling that it is losing power, will attempt some kind of scheme so that it can recoup its losses. In either case, whenever such a struggle takes place, it will be in the interest of somebody to exaggerate negative perceptions of an external enemy, either to hold on to what they have or to expand the scope of their holdings. In this way, the Soviet threat has achieved a position of prominence in American life whenever the equilibrium among the military branches has been upset.

Without question, the sharpest example of the relationship between military infighting and the exaggeration of anti-Soviet perceptions took place as the cold war began. World War II had made it clear that there would have to be some unification of the armed services, since the practice of giving each substantial autonomy tended to interfere with effective war planning. At the same time, all the traditional bureaucratic devices that prevent rational integration were sure to be pulled out if anyone seriously tried to bring a sense of order and planning to the fighting of wars. Caught between the military need for integration and the political realities that prevented it, policymakers sought a compromise. The National Security Act of 1947 gave them one. While unifying the services under a Secretary of Defense (and providing for a Joint Chiefs of Staff), it also allowed each of its own relative autonomy within the new structure. All that was accomplished, in other words, was to transfer the struggles from ones that took place between positions in the cabinet to ones that took place within one super-agency.[54]

These battles were exacerbated by the constituency politics that had developed over each service branch. The Navy Department, for example, tended to have its support among patrician families along the East Coast who, whether Republican or Democratic in sympathy, leaned toward strong leadership and the kind of active presidency symbolized by the Roosevelts (both former Secretaries of the Navy). James Forrestal, the first Secretary of Defense, was very much in this tradition. The Army, in contrast, was rooted in the South. Its politics tended to be Democratic (as benefitted a Southern institution). Moreover, because the Army was the most labor-intensive service, housing huge numbers of men from working class and poor backgrounds, it generally took an outlook on the world that was not ultra-reactionary. Army men often supported the welfare state and believed in the kind of active government that had characterized the U.S. since the New Deal.[55] Finally, the strength of the Air Force lay in the Far West, where exceptionally conservative politics and isolationism were strong. Most Air Force leaders were Republicans, tied to defense contractors that wanted to arm in a kind of Fortress America style, relying on huge, capital-intensive systems that carried with them enormous profits.

Both Franklin Roosevelt and Harry Truman had followed policies that tended to benefit the Army and the Navy at the expense of the Air Corps. But the Air Corps was convinced that the future belonged to airpower, for in the postwar period nuclear weapons were the number one reality, and it seemed as if the logical way to deliver such weapons was on airplanes. In addition, the burgeoning conservative sentiment and desire for normality that was a feature of the 1948-50 period worked to the advantage of the Air Corps, for it could offer the maximum protection at the least cost, fiscal and psychological. For all these reasons, the Air Corps began a campaign the moment the war ended to divorce itself from the Army and then to expand itself relative to its rivals. A commission headed by Thomas Finletter produced a report called *Survival in the Air Age* that trumpeted the virtues of a new service.[56] Support among scientists and intellectuals was won by the creation of the RAND corporation in California that was tied to the new service. Once created, the Air Force seemed determined to take control over the military establishment.

In their campaign for hegemony, prominent Air Force officials found themselves distorting the Soviet threat, for they needed a credible external enemy as a rationale for their campaign. Air Force General Carl Spaatz, who led the fight for his service, blithely stated the case as follows: "The low grade terror of Russia which paralyzes Italy, France, England, and Scandinavia can be kept from our own country by an ability on our part to deliver atomic destruction by air. If Russia does strike the U.S., *as she will if her present frame of mind continues,* only a powerful air force in being can strike back fast enough, and hard enough to prevent the utter destruction of our nation."[57] (Emphasis added). When a war scare broke out over Czechoslovakia in the spring of 1948, the Air Force saw its chance. Air Force Secretary Stuart Symington (one of the Democrats that had associated himself with the new service) created something called the 70-Group to lobby for greater funds for his service. He was successful. The military budget was entirely rewritten for FY 1949, and the share going to the Air Force had doubled. It had become clear to all how fanning the flames of an overseas crisis could be used to protect (and even expand) bureaucratic turf at home.

One important question remained unanswered: would the increase given to the Air Force be at the expense of the other

An Air Man's View
of the World

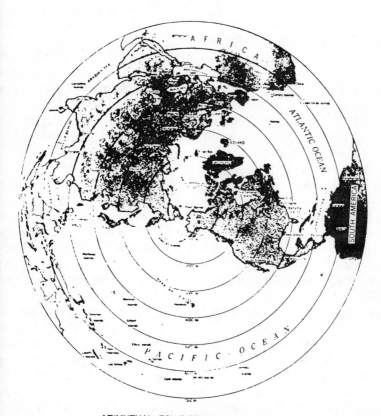

AZIMUTHAL EQUIDISTANT PROJECTION
CENTERED NEAR
POINT BARROW, ALASKA

This map, reproduced from *Survival in the Air Age,* graphically illustrates how small the world seems from the cockpit of a plane. The map makes it clear that the northern half of the world is more vital to the security of the U.S. than the southern. In that sense, the map attacks the Army's preference for intervention in southern Third World countries.

services? So long as the defense budget was held constant—which Truman was determined to do—then the obvious answer was yes. In this case, the other services had to find some way to protect their empires. One way was to highlight Soviet strength in a particular area, as the Navy had done the previous year when it argued that the Russian submarine fleet was stronger than Hitler's had been. But when the Navy lost its campaign for a flash-deck carrier in 1949,[58] it began to emphasize the overall threat from the Soviet Union rather than the specific threat posed by particular weapons. In that way, there would be enormous pressure on Truman to raise the ceiling that he had imposed on the military budget as a whole. With the ceiling lifted, the Air Force's gains would not be taken out of the hides of the other services.

The Air Force had shown how one service branch, trying to solidify its hegemony over the others, could use an exaggeration of the Soviet threat to achieve its purposes. By the late 1950s, as the second peak of anti-Soviet belligerency was building up, the Army began to show how a branch that was losing power could also use the Soviet threat in order to regain its prestige. Strengthened by vastly increased budgets, the Air Force had become more complacent during the 1950s, convinced that the discovery of nuclear weapons had made the other services obsolete. Although Eisenhower had been an Army man, he went along with this point of view, for his fiscal conservatism pushed him to support the Air Force's claim of a "bigger bang for the buck." So sure was the Air Force of its superiority that it failed to notice a rising challenge from a new generation of Army officers.

A cosmopolitan Army Chief of Staff named Maxwell Taylor launched a campaign during the closing years of the Eisenhower era to return the Army to its former position of prominence. Taylor was convinced of two things. First, though nuclear weapons were impressive, they were not likely to be used. Second, relying on them meant that the U.S. was becoming weaker, not stronger, for it was putting its military eggs in the wrong basket. Based upon these points, Taylor, in various Department of Defense internal memoranda and in his popular book *The Uncertain Trumpet*, urged the U.S. to build more conventional arms.[59] In addition, since any conflicts in Europe were likely to involve nuclear weapons (the stakes were that high), he urged that the U.S. think about areas of the world outside Europe, and especially about the Third World.

The only problem with Taylor's conception was that it was unclear how the interests of the United States were intertwined with the peripheral countries of the world. Latin America had

As the budgets rose during the 1960s, perceptions of the Soviet threat began to subside. With plenty of money to spend, no military service needed to sound the tocsin to obtain more.

always been a direct source of interest, but what role should the U.S. take toward countries in Asia, Africa and the Middle East? Eisenhower, and the Joint Chiefs, had specifically rejected an intervention into Vietnam in 1954 on the grounds that it was not worth the cost. To make it appear as if these countries were of vital and direct concern, Taylor and like-minded people claimed that the *real* enemy in such circumstances was the Russians. From this point of view, any revolution in the Third World was automatically a victory for the U.S.S.R. since it diminished the power and prestige of the United States.

Ironically, Taylor's view of the world gave the Russians more credit than they deserved. In the real world, the Russians were upset at the instability in the Third World and did not know what to make of all these nationalistic rebellions. But Taylor and other cold war enthusiasts like Walt Rostow, by seeing Russians everywhere, created a self-fulfilling prophecy. Since in their view the Russians *had* to be involved, then for all intents and purposes, the U.S. acted as if they were, whether they were or not. Direct U.S. intervention in the Third World would have to increase, as would the role of the Army, the most appropriate service for counter-insurgency warfare.

Kennedy, as a Democrat, leaned toward the Army view of events. He made Taylor a major figure in his administration. He increased the budget of the Army. He sponsored the notion of counter-insurgency warfare around which the Army was staging its comeback. In short, domestic political considerations—especially the link between the Army and the Democratic Party—had much to do with the attractiveness of a new strategic theory in the early 1960s. Since no new theory could be implemented without a revised (and revived) version of the Soviet threat, the Soviet threat was duly revised (and revived). From now on, the Russians were seen as wanting to expand into the Third World in exactly the same way an earlier generation viewed them as anxious to get their hands on France and Germany.

Kennedy also talked a great deal about bringing the

Department of Defense under control. Under Robert Mc-Namara's secretaryship, cost accountants, engineers, and systems analysts took over the Pentagon budget and announced that only cost-effective programs would be approved. Had this actually taken place, the military men would have been at each other's throats. In actuality, McNamara greatly expanded the overall military budget, and relative peace was brought to the war among the service branches. As the budgets rose during the 1960s, perceptions of the Soviet threat began to subside. With plenty of money to spend, no military service needed to sound the tocsin to obtain more.

The costs of bringing peace to Washington's inter-service rivalry were enormously high, as all participants realized. Furnishing each service with its own pet projects brought about the reality feared by conservatives since 1946: deficit spending, high taxes, and uncontrollable inflation. Indeed, by the time Nixon was elected, the economy seemed almost completely out of control, and at least one prominent reason for its erratic behavior was the drain that defense spending, especially but not exclusively in Vietnam, had upon domestic economic performance. Vietnam also diverted funds from Soviet-oriented services like the Strategic Air Command, leading them to revise the spectre of the Soviet threat in order to make a come-back.

How to Combat Inter-Service Rivalry

"The greater our variety of weapons, the more political choices we can make in any given situation."

John F. Kennedy (1961)

Nixon began to realize that some attempt to make choices in national defense would have to be made. Although military men think of themselves as apolitical creatures, interested not in partisanship but only in the national defense, the pattern since 1950 shows that the Army tends to fare better under Democrats and the Air Force under Republicans. As the following chart reveals, the Air Force budget increased (and the Army budget decreased) after 1953 when Eisenhower became president; this

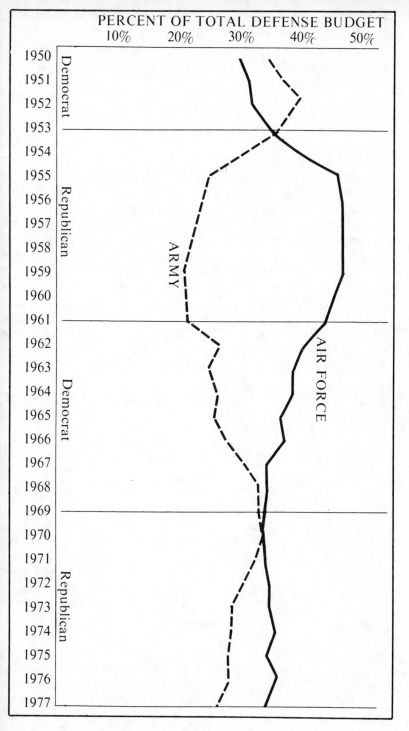

PERCENT OF TOTAL DEFENSE BUDGET

ARMY

AIR FORCE

pattern was reversed under Kennedy and Johnson; and it reversed again under Nixon and Ford.

Strategic theory was altered to account for the increased importance of the Air Force under Nixon. Maxwell Taylor's emphasis on guerilla wars was played down in favor of a direct counting of strategic weapons between the Soviet Union and the United States. Nixon's Secretaries of Defense repudiated McNamara's notion of Mutually Assured Destruction in favor of doctrines that emphasized the ability of the United States to destroy Soviet life. These new doctrines were far more compatible with the Air Force's outlook on the world than they were with the Army's.

If this interpretation of inter-service rivalry is correct, then Carter, once he become president, would be tempted to try and restore the Army's position. This seems to be the pattern that is developing. Unlike Nixon and Ford, Carter cancelled deployment of the B-1 bomber, although Congress has tried to keep alive the possibility of its revival. More importantly, both in PRM-10 and in his budgets, Carter has attempted to give a more prominent role to conventional weapons, which remain the preserve of the Army. (Indeed, the SALT II treaty, by limiting strategic weapons generally built by the Air Force, will enable the Administration to expand conventional arms built by the Army.) By identifying the Middle East as a crucial problem area, Carter is relying on lightening-quick deployment of tanks and helicopters, not massive nuclear weapons delivered from planes that fly in the stratosphere. Not surprisingly, Army men are pleased by these developments; representatives of the other two services are not as happy.

The Navy has been excluded the most from recent weapons choices, and as a result, Navy men have been making some of the more extreme versions of the Soviet threat, in particular Admiral Elmo Zumwalt. The same is true of the Air Force, even though it has been less hurt than the Navy. Loss of the B-1 was a bitter blow to the Air Force, which is also losing its hegemony due to changing technologies (like the obsolescence of manned strategic bombers in general). To some extent, the Air Force has recouped its losses through the cruise missile, the M-X, and the necessity to have airlift support for quick-strike conventional wars. But deprivation is always relative. Even though the Air Force has gained some new systems, it concentrates on the ones it has lost, and this gives it an incentive to join in the rising negative perception of the Soviet intentions. Thus, one of the leading proponents of the Team B offensive that is in the forefront of the third peak in anti-Soviet belligerence is retired Air Force General

George Keegan. His role has been crucial, leading a one-man crusade to convince America that the Soviet Union is obtaining nuclear superiority over the United States.

Kennedy's solution to a similar problem had been to expand the military budget so that the Army could have what it wanted without offending the Air Force. Carter seems to be adopting the same approach, even though the state of the domestic economy makes it more difficult to do so. He has promised the Air Force the M-X missile, which goes far to mute criticism of his policies from that direction. He wants an overall spending increase so that the Navy (Carter is a Navy man and identifies with that service) and the Army do not fall behind as a result. In short, an expanded military budget—whatever the cost in reduced social services—still constitutes the best way to avoid inter-service rivalry and with it, to attempt to quell the charge that a Democratic president is being "soft" on defense.

To summarize, the following relationships seem worth emphasizing:

1. Anti-Soviet perceptions will tend to rise when there is no rough balance between the military services in terms of their relative shares of the budget and one or another service seeks to enhance its relative position as a result.

2. Equilibria tend to break down when a new political party enters the White House. Traditionally, Democrats favor the Army, while Republicans incline toward the Air Force. (The Navy has advocates in both parties but, historically, has been associated with the "moderate" wing of the Republican Party, now almost obliterated.)

3. The most time-honored way of reetablishing an equilibrium among the service branches is to expand the overall military budget. Thus a recurrent pattern emerges: a new party comes to power; that party then shifts money toward its favorite service; those branches that stand to lose will "discover" the Soviet threat and issue harrowing warnings about America's future; at this point, presidents back off from confrontation (not wanting to appear weak in the face of an external threat); as they back off, the budget begins to climb, a new equilibrium is established, and the most negative perceptions of the Soviet Union begin to taper off.

Chapter VI:
Foreign Policy Coalitions and the Soviet Threat

To this point, my explanation for the peaks in anti-Soviet perceptions has concentrated exclusively on domestic politics, as if events taking place in the rest of the world were irrelevant. Those events must be included in any such analysis, as I will begin to do in this chapter. But, interestingly enough, many of the debates over foreign policy that influence perceptions of the U.S.S.R. have little to do with Russia directly. Indeed, anti-Soviet perceptions often become a tactic for winning support for attempts to reorient foreign policy toward totally different parts of the world.

In a democratic society like the United States, foreign policy cannot simply be made directly by a small elite unconcerned about interest groups or public opinion. It is necessary to build a coalition of interests around a specific foreign policy, and to win public support for that policy through mass appeals. Such talks are not easy, for highly divergent economic, ideological, and partisan disagreements exist about what the main locus of U.S. foreign policy should be. In this chapter I will argue that negative perceptions of Soviet conduct are an important device by which certain kinds of foreign policy coalitions try to win support for a change in the locus of U.S. foreign policy. More specifically, I will argue that the first peak in anti-Soviet hostility was related to an attempt by a European-oriented elite to shift policy away from a pro-Asian direction; that the second peak involved an attempt by foreign policy activists concerned with the Third World to reorient policy in that direction; and that the third potential peak has much to do with attempts to form a new foreign policy coalition in the wake of America's defeat in Vietnam. In short, the underlying point of this chapter is that foreign policy is relevant to understanding the rise and fall of the Soviet Union, but it is not always foreign policy toward Russia; negative perceptions of Soviet conduct become *instrumental* tactics designed to achieve other ends.

One of the most important disagreements within the foreign policy establishment until the late 1940s was between Europhiles, who thought of Europe as the quintessence of Western Civilization, and Asia-firsters, who were concerned about bringing "civilization" to the East. Asia-firsters tended to be tied to businessmen interested in expanding into new markets and territories.[60] They possessed an outlook on the world, and a location in the structure of production, that was quite different from those oriented toward Europe. Generally associated with new and more competitive industries located in the West, they were conservative in their politics, and were suspicious of the use of big government for any purpose other than protecting U.S. businessmen through tariffs. When they thought of overseas expansion, they envisioned business being free to move anywhere around the globe in the search for markets. Since European markets had been tied up for centuries, they generally viewed the Third World avariciously, and typically had a special interest in Asia, where more potential consumers exist than anywhere else. If they had had their way, American foreign policy would have been characterized by substantial help for business expansion; low military budgets except when absolutely necessary; a reluctance to endorse foreign aid; and a suspicion of permanent treaties, covert action, and other ways by which the U.S. could become entrapped in the internal wranglings of other countries, especially European ones.

European-oriented policymakers viewed the Asia-firsters roughly the way box holders at the opera think of wrestling fans. Generally men of considerable hereditary wealth, long since removed from the nitty-gritty of making money, the Europhiles were concerned with long-term global stability, not immediate profit. With ties to both the financial world and the monopoly sector—and with a domestic ideology that stressed long term reform in the interests of preserving the system as a whole—these men were far more sympathetic to using the power of government to organize the world than their Asian inclined colleagues. They thought of the world in terms of nation states, not specific business firms, and they wanted to see the American state be the unsurpassed power in the world. This meant a tolerance for high defense budgets, a standing army, support for foreign aid and covert intelligence, and a positive penchant for becoming involved in the affairs of other countries. To them, the ideal world would be one in which all Americans willingly shouldered the responsibilities of global leadership and permitted class-conscious State Department planners to seek peace through balance-of-power policies.[61]

Underlying the debate between the Asia-firsters and the Euro-capitalists were differences in economics that made the issues so bitter. The latter group tended to be free traders. In their view, capital should be free to move around wherever it can be most

63

efficient, regardless of national boundaries. But they also understood that no system of free trade and currency convertability could work unless one state were powerful enough to enforce it, as Britain had been able to do in the nineteenth century. The pro-European vision asked for domestic sacrifice in the name of long term patterns of growth in the world economy. Inefficient American industries would have to fold if they could not compete on world markets. Jobs at home might have to be sacrificed to protect capital mobility. The U.S. would have to accept balance--of-payment problems if they were necessary to rebuild Europe. In short, the economic program of the large corporations and financial interests that supported the Europe-firsters called for a denial of immediate gratification, not only on the part of labor, but also on the part of competitive-sector business. It was a program that, by itself, could never have attracted much mass appeal, especially in a country like the United States that had a long protectionist history.

Opposition to the free trade principles of the European-oriented elite came, not unexpectedly, from nationalistic businessmen that needed protection to compete on the world's markets, from labor unions that wanted to protect their members' jobs, and from all those people who, for whatever reason, did not want their tax dollars propping up other governments around the world. Economic nationalism, in addition, had far more popular appeal than free trade liberalism. It did not ask for sacrifices. It put the needs of Americans first. It spoke of an identity of interests between capitalists and workers in keeping business at home. It was, in short, the more "democratic" alternative in the sense that its popularity was, from the beginning, inherently greater.

Throughout most of the twentieth century, the Asia-first mentality had had substantial influence on American policy, from the acquisition of the Philippines in 1898 to the furor over the "loss" of China in the 1950s. Even as Hitler invaded country after country in the late 1930s, the strong and unbreakable Asia-first mentality prevented Franklin Roosevelt from intervening on the side of the European democracies. It was not until an Asian power, Japan, bombed an installation in the Far West, Pearl Harbor, that enough consensus existed in the United States to support the war effort. When World War II began, in other words, the Asia-first mentality was still in a superior position to the Europeanists.

A significant number of State Department officials hoped that the coming of World War II would prevent the U.S. from ever again returning to its anti-European proclivities. As the war came to an end, they were determined to find a way to preserve their emphasis on Europe as the center of both world civilization and of American concern abroad.

Numerous problems stood in the path of the Eurocapitalists in 1945. For one thing, the Asia-first sentiment, held in check during the war, was bound to explode once Germany and Japan had been defeated. Part of the right-wing counterattack after the war would surely involve the direction of U.S. foreign policy. In addition, the key to a stable Europe was Germany, yet the U.S. had just fought a major war against the Germans. In order for the Europeanists to have their way, Germany would have to be transformed from enemy to friend, and in the quickest possible time.

Beyond these problems, conditions in Europe were rather depressing to the Europeanists. The war-devastated economies of the continent would be unable to recover without American help. Yet there was not much sympathy in America for providing that assistance. Many people in Congress felt that if Europe was unable to defend itself, the U.S. should stay out of its affairs. Massive aid programs would only entangle the United States in situations that it could not control and lead the country, once again, into war.

In the late 1940s, negative images of Soviet expansionism became the device by which free trade liberals were able to overcome the inherently elitist aspects of their program and to sell it as having general appeal. By combining the free trade vision with the Soviet threat, the Europhiles were able to characterize protectionists and Asia-firsters as short-sighted, selfish, and uncharitable in the face of the world's problems. They were also being accused of being stingy on matters of national defense and of encouraging war and aggression. So long as the debate was posed in this fashion, the European-oriented free traders could dominate it, something they could never have been able to do without the Soviet threat. Thus the Russians were used to make a free trade program acceptable in a democratic society.

The first test of the political clout of the two foreign policy factions came in 1946 as the U.S. Congress considered a massive loan to the British. Conservative opposition, led by Ohio Senator Robert Taft, was fierce. Congressional leaders told Truman that the only way to pass the bill was to make a strongly anti-Soviet speech claiming that Britain's future was in danger from the Russians. Truman said no. Congressional leaders made the claim in any case, and the loan passed. Within two years, Truman would no longer be so reticent.[62]

The British loan, as conservatives correctly charged, was a

foot-in-the-door for more elaborate aid proposals. European-oriented policymakers had in mind an audacious plan to reconstruct the entire economy of Western Europe with an aid program so vast that capital flows around the world would be permanently altered. When the idea was unveiled at Harvard University by Secretary of State George Marshall, the opposition mobilized. Passage of the Marshall Plan, most policymakers realized, would so commit the U.S. to the future of a capitalist Europe that there would be no turning back.

The Marshall Plan was, in the end, approved by Congress. But Truman had been forced to pay a price. No longer could he refuse, as he had done with the British Loan, to arouse the spectre of the Soviet threat. Like the Air Force, Truman opted to manipulate domestic perceptions of the crisis in Czechoslovakia in February 1948 in order to build support for his program. NSC-68, which was Top Secret, had pointed out that the U.S. expected the Soviets to control Czechoslovakia and that the February crisis did not bring about any change in the balance of power. But that was for private consumption only. In public, the Truman Administration charged that a freedom-loving country had been invaded by totalitarianism for the second time in a decade. Even though U.S. officials had concluded that Czechoslovakia had already been a communist state before February 1948 (they had refused on that ground to give it foreign aid, for example, thereby insuring greater popularity for the Russians in that country), the solidification of Russian control became instrumental in reshaping domestic politics within the United States. The Marshall Plan was passed after Truman delivered a war scare speech in March.

This was no one-time-only piece of legislation. For the Marshall Plan to be effective in rebuilding European capitalism, a long term commitment to aid was necessary. For this reason, passage of the Marshall Plan did not quell the rhetoric of the Soviet threat but institutionalized it. Now there would have to be proof every year of the evil designs of the Kremlin (and the efficacy of foreign aid in stymying those designs) before renewal monies would be forthcoming. As Europe began its economic miracle, some of the more extreme rhetoric did relax, but further innovations in U.S.-Europe relations—particularly the NATO treaty and support for European integration—required the cultivation of negative images of Soviet intentions in order to pass through a Congress that still looked longingly on the Far East and suspiciously at Europe.[63]

These events show that the first peak in anti-Soviet hostility did have a foreign policy dimension, but one that was not exclusively concerned with the Soviet Union. To be sure, Russia was part of Europe and American policymakers were genuinely concerned about the threat posed by the Soviet Union to our European allies. But at the same time, a significant number of policymakers were more directly interested in building up the economic might of Europe, especially Germany, and the fear of the Soviets was to them an instrument to achieve this alternative objective. The events surrounding the Marshall Plan and the development of a free trade economy are an excellent illustration of how anti-Soviet perceptions became essential to foreign policy objectives that are tangential to a *direct* concern with the Soviet Union.

Events taking place in the real world are also related to the second peak of anti-Soviet hostility, although once again they involve U.S.-Soviet relations only tangentially. The activists that came to power with Kennedy were concerned with changing Eisenhower's priorities in two ways. First, while they were satisfied that a pro-European inclination had been adopted, they were concerned that it was not strong enough. Second, and more important, they wanted to shift American policy to a greater involvement with revolutions taking place in the Third World. Exaggerating the danger posed by the Russians became instrumental to both of these purposes.

During the 1950s, the Asia-firsters made an attempted comeback under Senator Joseph McCarthy, who tried to purge the State Department of its European orientation and led an attack on the China experts that, to him, were not sufficiently enraptured by the anti-communists in that part of the world. As a result, the pro-European policies adopted in the late 1940s were in danger. In addition, some Europeans, like DeGaulle, were showing disturbing signs of independence, and the economic costs of the pro-Europe alliance was high, as measured by balance of payments deficits that started to increase during the 1950s.

The sense of urgency about Europe that captivated Kennedy's advisors was reinforced by their perception that under Eisenhower the alliance had begun to atrophy. In the view of the

Kennedy men, Eisenhower had made needless concessions to the Soviets in 1959 over Berlin and was going to make more at the 1960 summit. This, they argued, was weakening American resolve, and, as a first order of business, the new administration should put the Russians on notice that the U.S. would not back down on its commitment to West Berlin. In March and May of 1961, Kennedy made bold speeches promising greater U.S. rearmament, directed principally against the Russians. His advisor, Dean Acheson, called for an explicit confrontation with the Russians over Berlin, and Kennedy was willing to listen.[64] Facing all this, Khrushchev upped the ante and threatened to sign a separate peace treaty with East Germany. The stage was set for a confrontation over Europe, a situation that Eisenhower had tried to avoid. Kennedy went to Berlin and announced that he was a Berliner. The Soviets put up a wall, a concrete symbol of the bankruptcy of their own policies.[65] One effect of all these moves was to restore a European consciousness to American affairs. More military aid went to NATO, troop commitments to Germany increased, and the military alliance between the U.S. and Western Europe was solidified.

But equally as important to the Kennedy Administration as the firming up of the European alliance was its concern with the Third World. In Asia and Africa, newly independent countries were coming into existence every year. Populous, strategically important, and loaded with raw materials, these countries were clearly going to play a major role in future international politics. The West's policy toward the Third World had been a colonial one, which did not make much sense for the last half of the twentieth century. The Kennedy Administration took the lead in trying to fashion a policy that would be more appropriate to this new reality than the simple business-dominated neo-colonialism of the Eisenhower Administration.

Kennedy's thinking on the Third World was heavily influenced by a group of intellectuals in Cambridge, Massachusetts who had been studying the revolutionary movements in those countries. These men—Walt Rostow, Lincoln Gordon, McGeorge Bundy, Lucian Pye, and others—argued that the best policy for the United States was to encourage "economic development" in these countries, to offer them a non-communist path to wealth and power.[66] Such a program meant substantial economic aid to build up the infrastructure of these countries—roads, education, water projects, etc.—and heavy military aid to protect regimes favorable to the United States. Their program also implied covert operations that would insure "stability." In short, they asked for substantial U.S. involvement in "development," coupled with

Selling the Threat to the Third World

It is of great importance that the American people, now well aware of the technical and scientific challenge posed by the Communist world, understand and rise to meet the equally great, and perhaps more subtly dangerous, offensive which the Sino-Soviet bloc has vigorously launched in the less developed areas. This offensive represents an attempt by the Sino-Soviet bloc to employ its growing economic and industrial capacities as a means of bringing the newly developing free nations within the Communist orbit.

C. Douglas Dillon, Deputy Undersecretary of State for Economic Affairs, speaking in 1958. Dillon, who would become Kennedy's Treasury Secretary, would seem to be exaggerating, since the "Sino-Soviet bloc" was actually, at the time he spoke, beginning to fall apart.

heavy military aid to pro-U.S. governments designed to insure the "climate of stability" needed for development.

There were numerous problems with the developmental approach, the most important being that the very trade and currency policies being followed by the U.S. were reinforcing "underdevelopment."[67] From a political standpoint another problem was even more severe. There was no domestic political coalition within the United States that was favorable to a massive program of foreign aid. Indeed, latent American isolationism, very strong in Congress, had insured the failure of any attempts by the Eisenhower Administration to provide aid in a consistent form. Unable to sell their program on its own merits (who could make a convincing case for Congress that foreign aid was not a massive "give-away"?), Kennedy's advisors discovered that their program was politically feasible only under one condition. If they could prove to Congress (and to the American people) that these countries were imperiled by Soviet "aggression," then the required political support for a program of foreign aid might be forthcoming. No wonder that talk of Soviet expansion became so much louder during this period.

Kennedy's approach was, by and large, successful. Foreign aid was significantly expanded, new programs like the Alliance for Progress were established, and American foreign policy became more and more intertwined with Third World concerns. Indeed, by the end of the Kennedy-Johnson Administrations, U.S. policy was so focused on Southeast Asia that a number of eminent Europhiles, the most typical being George Ball, had come out against the Vietnam policy because it was distracting the U.S. from its primary commitment: Western Europe. But Ball's was a voice in wilderness; more typical of the Kennedy-Johnson Administrations were men like Walt Rostow. Rostow, who had taken the lead among intellectuals in arguing that the U.S.S.R. was the main threat to the Third World,[68] failed to see that the Russians were more concerned with stability than with revolution. The Soviets were suspicious of Castro, critical of the Algerian revolution, doubtful about the possibilities of revolutionary change in Venezuela, opposed to "adventurism" all around the world, and ultimately would become hostile to China. In other words, there was precious little evidence that the Russians were actively fomenting revolt in the Third World, but it was important to convey that impression in order to win domestic support for a shift in American foreign policy objectives. In the end, Rostow and his compatriots were worried that revolutions in the Third World might close off U.S. access to resources as much as they were concerned about Russian expansion.

The second peak of anti-Soviet hostility, like the first, had a foreign policy dimension, but not one directly related to U.S.-Soviet relations. Fear of the Russians was exaggerated in order to win support for foreign aid and a Third World orientation, just as, in the first phase, it was helpful in winning support for the Marshall Plan and a European orientation. The two peaks are not similar in terms of the specific focus of foreign policy, but they are quite similar in terms of the way that negative perceptions of Soviet conduct helped build domestic support for a shift in foreign policy orientation.

Recent attempts by organizations like the Committee on the Present Danger to warn of an imminent Soviet threat to the United States are related to yet another shift in the locus of foreign policy, this one a result of the breakdown of the foreign policy consensus symbolized by Vietnam, combined with attempts by the Nixon Administration to redirect policy away from Europe.

Nixon's administration had been a nightmare for the Europeanists. As a legislator, Nixon had been an important cog in the Asia-first machine. His roots were in California, where Europeanist inclinations had never been strong. Even though Nixon had been "seasoned" with a New York law practice, there was no guarantee that he would accept the legacy of the Marshall Plan outlook on the world.

In three significant ways, Nixon attempted to break U.S. policy away from the Eurocapitalist vision. First, he wondered aloud about the relevance of NATO. Europe, and the Europeanists, were shocked by Henry Kissinger's "Year of Europe" speech in 1973, in which he noted that the "United States has global interests and responsibilities. Our European allies have regional interests."[69] Kissinger was calling for a relaxation of America's preoccupation with Europe in favor of an outlook that made Europe simply one area of concern among many.

Secondly, Nixon did, in fact, apply the Asia-first mentality while president, albeit with a catch. Nixon's opening with China was proof of his determination to upgrade Asia in the strategic thinking of the United States. If one simply ignores the fact that China is governed by Communists, which Nixon in his new found ideological eclecticism was willing to do, then the new China policy was nothing other than the right-wing approach of the 1940s brought to life. China had finally been called upon to play the role that the China Lobby had demanded, only it was not the China of Chiang Kai-shek.

Finally, Nixon's foreign economic policies repudiated all the crucial notions of the Europeanists. In 1971 Nixon suspended the Bretton Woods agreements that had organized the postwar world, and took the U.S. off the gold standard. Moreover, Nixon's Secretary of the Treasury, John Connally, was an unabashed economic nationalist who favored protectionist policies and a go-it-alone mentality. Neither the integrationists of the Common Market nor the free-traders in the multinational corporations were happy with Nixon's attempt to insure the self-sufficiency of the American economy at whatever the international economic costs.

As if this was not enough, American foreign policy was in even greater disarray because of the fallout from the Vietnam War. It would seem to be true, as Leslie Gelb had argued, that Vietnam followed logically from the policies of containment elaborated during the 1940s.[70] For this very reason, the U.S. failure in that country was extremely serious, for it raised the question of whether or not containment itself was flawed. Did the U.S. "need" to commit so much to Vietnam? If one accepted the idea that the Russians were behind every Third World revolution, and that this "aggression" constituted a threat to U.S. security, then Vietnam was logical and necessary. Many experts, such as Walt Rostow, still feel that it was the right war at the right time. But if one rejects the vital interest of Vietnam to American security—as men like Clark Clifford and Paul Warnke implicitly did—then one also rejects some of the crucial components of the entire containment strategy.

The American withdrawal from Vietnam began a major debate in policymaking circles about the future locus of foreign policy. Some argued that only "core" areas of direct vital concern to the U.S.—especially Europe and the Middle East—required military intervention, while other areas like Africa were not worth the cost. Others argued that Vietnam was a failure of nerve on the part of the U.S., demanding an even greater commitment to the principles of cold war liberalism. The debate became extremely heated, and it burst into the public arena when the Carter Administration took office in 1977. Carter seemed to side with the position that emphasized a commitment only to the core areas, and that aroused the ire of all those who believed that the problem in Vietnam was a failure of American will.

The Carter Administration came into power with two apparent objectives: restoring Europe to its proper place after Nixon and developing a new U.S. stance vis-a-vis the Third World after Vietnam. The former task was urged most prominently by the Trilateral Commission, the ultimate in pro-European sympathies and close to the Carter Administration in outlook and personnel.[71] The program of the Trilateralists represents a return to the free trade principles of the late 1940s; a solidification of the NATO alliance; the creation of a new system of trade and currency to replace Bretton Woods and to supplement international trade negotiations; support for European integration; and a search for areas in which North America, Europe, and Japan can overcome petty national disputes in favor of international cooperation. It seems like Europe versus Asia once again, only this time Japan is seen as part of the European alliance. But it is not, for the domestic coalitions have shifted greatly since the late 1940s. This shift helps explain both why Carter's foreign policy is failing and why the anti-Soviet perceptions are increasing.

If recent American history shows anything, it is that it is difficult to have a free trade oriented program without the cultivation of the Soviet threat, for such a program hurts all those Americans who lose jobs and income overseas and runs counter to chauvinistic prejudices. Only if people are convinced that an overwhelming danger exists from abroad can their support for economic harm be won. Therefore, if the Trilateralists were to be successful, they would have to cultivate some of the images of Soviet totalitarianism. There has been some of this; one report of the Trilateral Commission did revivify all the 1940s language

The Return of the Europeanists

. . . the United States government has preferred in the last few years to deal bilaterally with individual European governments and Japan, and to centralize relations on itself, as in the past, believing that this maximized its power and prolonged its leadership . . .

But the drawbacks of bilateralism are great. It is not surprising that the Japanese and Europeans, though of great potential importance to each other, both in themselves and in the effect they have on America, have very little sense of each other or their potential role together in the international system. The necessary development of a Europe able to speak with a single voice is made more difficult. And the United States is encouraged to underrate its partners' adaptations to a changing context. It sees itself all too easily as the only power with an adequate world view, an attitude which buttresses its unilateralism and desire to maintain the privileges of leadership, even when it is less and less able to exercise leadership responsibilities by itself . . .

It is in this spirit that the Trilateral Commission, with participants from North America, Japan and the European Community, has been set up to propose jointly considered contributions by their nations to the major international issues that confront mankind.

Trilateral Commission, *The Crisis of International Cooperation* (1973)

---

about Soviet expansion. But, by and large, the Carter Administration has been unwilling to adopt without qualification the most extreme anti-Soviet perceptions. The reason has a good deal to do with the other foreign policy item on Carter's agenda: developing a post-Vietnam strategy for the Third World.

The pro-Europeanists around Carter—such as Cyrus Vance—are convinced that the U.S. overextended itself in Vietnam. They are strong believers in the notion that the U.S. should concern itself most explicitly with core areas like the Middle East and rely on non-interventionary solutions in other parts of the world, especially Africa. Their problem, therefore, is as follows. If they arouse the spectre of the Soviet threat, they put themselves in the

position where they will be forced to intervene in areas not o
their choosing, like Angola or Iran. They are on the horns of a
dilemma. They need the Soviet threat for their European policy
but if they adopt it, they undermine their own Third World
policy. No wonder they seem so confused and uncertain.

The contradictions of the Carter Administration give right
wing critics an open field to capture anti-Soviet sentiment. They
understand that Carter is vulnerable and have been pushing him
to the limit. But the right has its own contradictions. Groups like
the Committee on the Present Danger, composed mostly o
Democrats, contain disaffected Europeanists like Paul Nitze
who agrees with Carter that Europe is the center of the world bu
disagrees with him over the means to preserve it. Meanwhile, the
more orthodox right wing, men like General Keegan and
organizations like the Coalition for Peace Through Strength
seem like old Asia-firsters. They are willing to attack the Carte
Administration for its failures in Europe but their main preoc
cupation is elsewhere. If this anti-communist coalition were to
come to power, these differences would become much stronger

Thus, since 1976 the political coalitions have criss-crossed
making it difficult to distinguish all the participants along a
simple Europe versus Asia dimension. This criss-crossing is one
reason why the third peak of anti-Soviet hostility has not reached
its full heights. No longer is it possible to fan the flames of the
Soviet menace in order to win support for a pro-Europe policy
There are contradictions everywhere, giving no faction a
monopoly on the Soviet threat. As a result, negative perception
of Soviet intentions do not ring out as clearly as they did during
the two previous peak periods.

These reflections suggest that while foreign policy issues are
important to understanding the rise and fall of negativ
perceptions of Soviet conduct, they are not always issues that
directly concern the Soviet Union. Distilling the debates over th
orientation of U.S. foreign policy produces the following
conclusions:

1. Negative perceptions of Soviet intentions increase when
existing foreign policy coalitions are in disarray and, when new
coalitions seek to push foreign policy in a new direction.

2. The first peak of anti-Soviet sentiment was related to
attempts to give American foreign policy a European orien
tation; the second peak was part of a campaign to enhance the
importance of the Third World; and the last is a product of the
collapse of the cold war liberal consensus after Vietnam and
Nixon. But in all three cases it was the domestic side to the foreign

policy coalition that was responsible for the increase in the perception of the Soviet threat, not specific aspects of U.S.-Soviet relations.

3. In general, the threat from the Soviet Union is seen as more serious by the side in the foreign policy debate that has a more elitist program. Free-traders, who offer less immediate protection for jobs and capital, often find that the fear of an external enemy gives their economic program some legitimacy.

4. At the present time, domestic coalitions over foreign policy have criss-crossed so much that there is substantial confusion in foreign policy circles. This may explain why the third wave of anti-Soviet sentiment is less unified than the previous two.

Chapter VII:
Economic Transformations and Anti-Soviet Hostility

Numerous theories have been proposed about the relationship between the defense budget and the economy. Paul Baran and Paul Sweezy, for example, argue that huge defense expenditures are necessary to absorb the "surplus" generated by capitalism, which produces much more than it can consume and therefore requires tremendous waste.[72] Seymour Melman, on the other hand, maintains that defense spending is a drain on economic growth, that far from being necessary (as Baran and Sweezy imply), it is not in the best interests of American capitalism.[73] Other writers argue that imperialism is essential to the performance of the American economy, and that the maintenance of an imperial system requires large-scale defense expenditures whatever the state of the domestic economy.[74]

There are elements of truth to all these theories, but all of them are also static; they assume little variation in the pattern of defense spending. Yet, as I argued in Chapter II, negative perceptions of an external enemy rise and fall, and as they do, the size of the defense budget goes up and down. Therefore it is essential to determine whether there are similar economic transformations taking place during each of the peaks in anti-Soviet perceptions, and whether these periods are different from the two valleys. In this chapter, I will argue that the peak periods were times in which political coalitions were arguing for a strategy of macroeconomic growth and found the use of the defense budget the most political acceptable way of trying to effectuate that result.

First, it is worth noting that there is a relationship between overall economic conditions and the rise of the Soviet threat, but it is not the relationship that one might immediately expect. Negative perceptions of Soviet intentions generally peak after periods of recession, not during them.

In 1946, economists of every conceivable political stripe expected a letdown after the tremendous productive outpouring of World War II. Truman's economic advisors, especially activists like Leon Keyserling of the Council of Economic Advisors, saw defense spending as a good way to avoid the expected recession. Indeed, NSC-68, in which Keyserling and his

76

aides participated, recommended defense spending as a way of enhancing the economic growth of the United States. The only problem was that by the time NSC-68 was written, 1950, the postwar recessionary expectations had already passed. With the economy beginning its long postwar boom, the rise in defense spending that took place in the early 1950s was no longer "needed" to bring the country out of a trough.

Similarly, the books by Maxwell Taylor and Henry Kissinger that began the full-scale assault on Eisenhower's foreign policy and produced the second wave of anti-Soviet perceptions were published at a time when the economy had entered its biggest slowdown since the depression. Reluctant to follow an activist macroeconomic course, Eisenhower's domestic policymakers were most worried about inflation and attempted to cool down the economy when they concluded that economic growth was getting out of hand. By 1957, when the Taylor and Kissinger books were being written, the Eisenhower Administration had produced a situation in which both inflation and unemployment were high. The foreign policy activists that were so critical of Eisenhower's "New Look" pointed out that the economy would benefit from increased defense spending. Yet by the time they had an impact, in the first two years of the Kennedy Administration, the economy had recovered and was in the process of racking up its best growth record in the postwar period. Once again, increased expenditures for defense took place after the recession, not during it.

Recent experience also conforms to this pattern. Since 1968 there has been a substantial downturn in the American economy. For most of this time, while Republicans were president, slowed economic growth was not necessarily seen as a bad thing. There were some economists, however, who felt that the fall-off in defense spending under Nixon and Ford could not be allowed to continue. But even as the Carter Administration came into office and began to increase defense spending, the worst aspects of the recession had passed. A new recession is expected in 1980 or 1981, but it remains true that Carter's decision to upgrade the defense budget occurred after the previous recession had peaked in 1974.

Because increases in defense spending come after recessions, one cannot make a simple correlation between overall levels of economic performance and the rise and fall of anti-Soviet perceptions. It is true that the first tremors of a new build-up of hard-line views toward the Soviet Union occur during times of recession. But by the time that these sentiments are converted into higher defense expenditures, the "need" for the economic stimulant has passed. This suggests that one must enrich an economic understanding of the problem with a political analysis, that political economy, and not economics *per se*, helps explain the rise and fall of negative perceptions toward the Soviet Union.

Support for the cold war on the part of major manufacturers and large-scale labor unions has been close to axiomatic in the postwar period. A very strong political coalition that lobbies in favor of increased defense spending has come into existence, and, in order to make the case for a higher military budget, relies on the cultivation of an external threat. Indeed, sometimes the perceptions of a hostile enemy and the profits that accrue from the defense budget are so blatant as to be embarrassing. When both corporations and unions have a direct stake in the military budget, they cannot but make the claim that America needs a greater defense effort; it is economic suicide not to.

The fact that the military budget is an indirect means of sustaining profits and jobs is important to note, for it helps explain the persistence of anti-Soviet sentiments. But it does not explain why those sentiments rise and fall. The answer to that question lies in the nature of political coalitions that organize to promote economic growth.

One pattern that emerges in the first two peak periods of anti-Soviet hostility is that a governing coalition comes into power based upon promises to the working class, minorities, and other disadvantaged groups. Many politicians, especially Democrats, find that they must make such promises in order to be elected. Once in power, when faced with the choice of taking from the rich or trying to expand the whole pie, they invariably choose the latter, since it is politically more acceptable. And when they try to expand the size of the economy, they discover that the public budget is an important source of economic growth. Committing themselves to an expansion of the budget, they further discover that among the many ways to spend the public's money, defense spending is the least controversial. Unlike public housing or medical care, which arouse the ire of private companies that provide those services for profit, defense spending has no direct opposition in the private sector. Indeed the opposite is true, for defense spending has created a sector all its own which needs increased spending. Consequently, there is enormous pressure on politicians to stimulate macroeconomic growth by using the defense budget. Its purpose is not the short-term goal of taking the economy out of recession, but a future-oriented goal of sustaining a growth coalition organized around spending in order to expand the economy so that those at the bottom will be able to obtain more without detracting from the privileges of those at the top.

Alternatively, it is also clear that the valleys in hostility toward external enemies come when growth coalitions are not in power. Republican presidents generally do not make extensive promises to working class people and minorities about enhanced social benefits. They often try to campaign on the fear of inflation, which is of more direct concern to middle-class people, or on the basis of highly-symbolic, non-economic issues like crime or national prestige. Not having committed themselves to deliver on promises, the resulting coalitions need not fuel extensive economic growth. In fact, Republican coalitions often try to slow down the rate of growth in order to bring inflation under control. Thus they do not need nor want growth in the public budget, and they make an attempt to bring federal spending, including defense spending, under control. This also means lower taxes, an attractive campaign promise to the middle class. Under these conditions, negative perceptions of an external enemy would harm their economic program, for it would lead to macroeconomic stimulation that they are trying to avoid. No wonder that fear of an external enemy decreases under political coalitions that are opposed to federally sponsored macroeconomic growth.

Both the Truman and Kennedy periods confirm the relation between macroeconomic growth coalitions and the rise of the Soviet threat. Truman, for example, while personally not convinced of the notion that federal spending was good for the expansion of the economy, brought into policymaking circles Leon Keyserling, who believed in the idea very much. Keyserling was a domestic liberal who urged extensive governmental programs in housing and medical care. He was also a foreign policy activist who wanted to expand defense spending. (Keyserling is currently on the board of the Committee on the Present Danger.) When Truman's plans for public housing were scuttled by the real estate lobby and when his medical care plan was devastated by the American Medical Association, defense spending became the most attractive option to bring about continued economic growth. Keyserling, who was the second Chairman of the Council of Economic Advisors, wrote, along with his staff, the economic sections of NSC-68. That document noted that "The United States . . . is allocating only about 20 percent of its resources to defense and investment (or 22 percent including foreign assistance), and little of its investment outlays are directed to war-supporting industries. In an emergency the United States could allocate more than 50% of its resources to military purposes and foreign assistance, or five to six times as much as present."[75] This was a sign that increased federal spending on a vast scale was possible. Although Truman personally opposed so ambitious a program, the ground was laid for using the defense budget as a politically acceptable means of effectuating economic growth.

The situation had become clearer by the time that Kennedy took office. Kennedy's entire campaign had been oriented around a plea to move the country, which was generally interpreted as a plea for more rapid economic growth. There are two general ways to achieve such growth. One is for the government to create it by spending a great deal, sending ripples through the economy, and producing a multiplier effect that would lead to increased production. Few doubt that such a program works; the conservative argument against it is merely that the costs (inflation, inefficiency, whatever) would be greater than the benefits. Their alternative method is for the government to encourage business to invest more actively. Inducements such as tax cuts, subsidies, and favorable trade terms have generally been used toward that end.

Kennedy, as a centrist president, tried both approaches. Aware of those to his right, the president, particularly after his confrontation with the steel industry, "simply did not want another fight with business," as Arthur Schlesinger, Jr. has put it.[76] The question facing the Administration was how to achieve economic growth without antagonizing business. The president therefore chose to rely on indirect measures, such as a tax cut to stimulate consumer spending or an investment tax credit to urge business to invest.

But Kennedy could not rely on indirect measures only, for they do not have controllable impacts on overall growth levels. As a result, the new administration also paid attention to using the federal budget as an economic stimulant. This raised the opposition of business. But when big business denounced government spending, which it does reflexively, it announced opposition, not to spending *per se* (businessmen want federal spending that subsidizes them) but to programs that redistribute income. Defense spending, Kennedy discovered, is one of the few major spending programs that does not arouse business opposition—space exploration was another. Thus Kennedy was able to use government to stimulate economic growth without arousing conservative ire.

Defense spending has a variety of economic impacts. Generally, federal spending on defense works to the benefit of the largest firms. It also forces the economy to reorganize itself along advanced technological lines, to the advantage of those (already large) companies that can afford the costs of increasingly capital

80

Kennedy relied on defense spending to stimulate the economy because previous presidents had done so, making the defense production sector so powerful that no president can ignore it.

intensive machinery. In addition, the large outlays of federal monies encourage those who already have the greatest political power to try and take a larger share, thus favoring firms that have sufficient size to maintain a large Washington effort at lobbying. The impact of these centralizing tendencies is that each spurt of defense spending strengthens those non-market oriented monopolies that can mobilize themselves to push for a greater share of the *next* round of defense spending. In short, when the spectre of an external threat is raised in one period as a means of increasing defense spending, it lays the foundation for raising the same spectre in the next period. Kennedy relied on defense spending to stimulate the economy because previous presidents had done so, making the defense production sector so powerful that no president can ignore it.

When we turn to the present period, which I have characterized as an uncompleted peak in negative perceptions of the Soviet Union, we find the economic pattern more confused. On the one hand, President Carter faces a bloated defense sector that can make loud noises about any effort to curb its appetites. This predisposes Carter to want to increase the defense budget regardless of anything else taking place in any part of the world. But in addition, Carter ran for office with the support of blacks and union members. Having chosen not to support any new programs to keep their support, he needs to fashion economic growth as did Kennedy and Truman. He has, in opposition to his policies, an effective cold war liberal lobbying effort organized by men like Senators Jackson and Moynihan, who argue that the U.S. can still have both guns and butter. Under these conditions, the traditional response of using the defense budget to stimulate macroeconomic growth has some appeal, and Carter has responded with the usual cold war liberal attempts to raise the defense budget.[77]

But at the same time, economic conditions have changed drastically since the Kennedy Administration. There are substantial fiscal limitations on what the state can spend, which means that defense budget increases have to be paid for with reductions in all other services. In addition, exceptionally vicious inflation leads Carter in a traditional Republican direction, afraid of stimulating the economy and hoping for a recessionary slowdown that will halt rising prices. Finally, large defense budgets at this time would be harmful to the balance of payments, for it would result in shipping more goods and services overseas. Unlike the situation with Kennedy and Truman, Carter simply cannot rely on greater federal spending to stimulate economic growth. He is in a real bind economically, unable to move in any direction, and simply in a holding pattern hoping to be reelected.

Thus, while Carter from time to time invokes the Soviet threat in order to win support for his pledge to increase defense spending, he cannot invoke it too much, for a hasty spending spree on defense at this time would have substantially negative impacts on the American economy. This economic dilemma helps explain why Carter is more ambiguous about the Soviet threat than his Democratic predecessors. But it also helps explain why the traditional cold war liberals in the Committee on the Present Danger have the impact that they have had. Groups like the Committee, because they are not in power, face no economic restraints; they can raise the spectre of an external threat at will, without having to worry about the economic consequences that will follow from their pleas for enhanced national security. It is easy to claim that money is no object when one is not responsible for spending it. The Committee on the Present Danger's strategy is to reconstitute cold war liberalism as an effective governing strategy by forcing the issue of the Soviet threat back on the agenda, where a president like Carter cannot ignore it. It may be the case, however, that the Committee, should it ever come to power in the form of Jackson or Moynihan, would find itself facing the same kinds of fiscal limitations experienced by Carter.

Thus, it is possible to conclude that one must consider domestic economics in trying to explain why hostile perceptions of the Soviet Union increase at some times more than others, but the relationships are not direct and uncomplicated. They can be summarized as follows:

1. Often the first stirrings of a new wave of anti-Soviet perceptions will originate in recessionary times, or times when a recession is expected. But one cannot conclude from this that there is necessarily a direct intent to use the Soviet threat to increase the defense budget, for by the time the threat is translated into hard dollars, the recession has generally passed.

2. It is not the avoidance of recession but the attempt to create a

macroeconomic strategy of economic growth that best explains the rise of anti-Soviet perceptions. The perceived threat from the Soviet Union increases when activist domestic coalitions come to power. These coalitions have promised benefits to those on the lower end of the economic scale, which they hope to pay off through an overall expansion of the economy. (The alternative to expansion is taking from the higher rungs, which courts political danger.) As they search for politically safe measures of expanding the budget, such administrations inevitably discover the defense budget, for, unlike social welfare, defense spending does not redistribute income, and therefore does not arouse opposition from businessmen and conservatives. In this sense, increases in the perception of an external enemy are associated with attempts to raise the defense budget. Although it would be hard to trace a direct causal link between growth strategies and deliberate manipulation of perceptions of Soviet intentions, there are definitely periods in which economic needs and foreign policy perceptions work to support each other.

3. Alternatively, perceptions of the Soviet threat decline when an administration is in power that is not attracted to economic growth, for it has not made any promises to the poor and the powerless that it has to pay off. Indeed, if anything, such anti-growth coalitions fear a rise in foreign policy hostility, for that might mean inflationary budgets and the necessity to raise taxes.

4. When the economy is overtly contradictory, as it is at the present time, there is a likelihood that perceptions of an external enemy will be contradictory, as they are at the present time also.

Chapter VIII:
Meeting the Threat
From the Soviet Threat

The issue of whether the Soviet Union is a direct threat to the security of the United States is, as I pointed out in Chapter 1, the most important issue that the American public will have to decide in the near future. Americans are being told by organizations like the Committee on the Present Danger and the American Security Council that their way of life is in danger. President Carter has also from time to time warned of the danger posed by the Soviet Union, even as he urges ratification of a Strategic Arms Limitation Treaty with it. From all sides, the question of Soviet intentions is being once again placed on the American political agenda. What is the ordinary American to think?

Throughout this report I have argued that in many significant ways, the Carter period resembles the two previous peaks of anti-Soviet perceptions, although not as clearly. A Democrat, Carter is governing on foreign policy at the suffrance of the right, which seems to be calling the shots over such innovations as the Panama Canal treaty and SALT II. There was a substantial attack on the powers of the president as a result of Watergate, and one of the tasks of the Carter Administration is to restore some credibility to the idea of presidential power. Interservice rivalries are strong, both because of the advent of new technologies and because a fiscal crisis does not allow endless expansion of the military budget. A significant pro-European organization, the Trilateral Commission, urged the new administration to reorient foreign policy, and there is significant sentiment within the Carter Administration (and even stronger sentiment outside it) to intervene in Third World countries. And finally, a serious economic slowdown raises the possibility of reconstituting the macroeconomic growth coalition that hopes to fuel economic stimulation through federal spending.

If all the preconditions for a new wave of foreign policy belligerency exist, whether they produce concrete, aggressive actions on the part of the United States or just fade away after the SALT treaty can only be answered politically. If a strong left existed, a counterbalance to a new belligerency would operate. But without domestic opposition, movements toward a more anti-Soviet foreign policy will take on a certain air of inevitability.

Even though President Carter has been trying to hold the line on foreign policy, disturbing signs of an upward trend in belligerence are present. In 1946, by emphasizing the worst case analysis of Soviet motives, the U.S. guaranteed that the cold war would take place (this is not the same as "causing" the cold war). In 1980, the question is whether a new wave of cold war hostility can be prevented. In part to win support for SALT II, Carter has approved development of the M-X missile. Unlike a number of other systems, the M-X has significant first-strike capacity, that is, it can be used as an offensive weapon before any other country used weapons against the United States. For the Administration to commit itself to this and other similar weapons means a significant shift in strategic policy.[78] Its advocates argue that the Soviets are building a first-strike capability, forcing the U.S. to respond. But this is exactly what happened at the onset of the cold war, when ambiguity over Soviet intentions gave way to actions that brought about the very hostility that was being predicted. It is simply not true that the Soviets unquestionably are planning a first-strike capacity vis-a-vis the U.S. But it is true that if the U.S. develops one towards them, that they will try and develop another in return. *In this sense, the perception of Soviet intentions held within the U.S. at this time is of extraordinary importance, for if the most negative perceptions are upheld, a dangerous increase in nuclear tensions will follow.*

For this reason, America—in fact, the whole world—faces a clear and present danger from the Soviet threat. It is, however, not the threat from Russia that runs the risk of destroying democracy in the United States but the threat posed by those who would arm the United States to the teeth for reasons that have little to do with national security and much to do with politics. There are any number of powerful policymakers and institutions that would, in the name of preserving freedom, centralize political power in undemocratic ways; curtail civil liberties in order to protect them; create a highly monopolistic economy that would be inflationary and inefficient; suspend or cut back social welfare programs if they interfered with the defense budget; militarize American values; intervene throughout the world whenever they felt it justified; support the most racist regimes in order to protect us from communism; force the United States to resemble the authoritarian countries against which it is allegedly struggling; and develop dangerous new nuclear weapons that would destabilize the existing balance. It is vital, in my view, for the United States to find a way to protect itself against this threat.

Because there is such a substantial political core to the waxing and waning of the Soviet threat, the danger that America faces from within can only be met *politically*. The threat from those who try to exaggerate the Soviet threat will be met only when a political challenge has been issued to the dominant way that public business is conducted in the United States.

As I have tried to point out in this essay, the Soviet threat has become a regular feature of American life because it is essential to each of the following processes:

- it enables the Democratic Party to govern without developing a program for reorganizing social life along progressive lines, while protecting itself from the demagoguery of the right;
- it is a useful device to prop up the necessity of a strong executive in the face of popular feelings that political power should be broken up and kept weak;
- it has enabled bureaucratic vested interests—particularly in the military services—to retain their hold over the federal budget while other interests seek inroads into what they have
- it has been the method by which foreign policy coalition with unpopular ideas (free trade, extensive foreign aid) have mobilized public and interest group support for a shift in the locus of American foreign policy;
- finally, it has permitted advocates of greater economic growth to develop a method of stimulating the economy through federal spending without supporting controversial programs that would arouse opposition from business and conservative groups.

The way to meet the threat from the Soviet threat is to create a progressive political presence in the United States, one that can rectify the rightward tilt that exists on all foreign policy and defense issues. Contained in this unremarkable assertion are two imperatives. First, those who are attempting to build a progressive coalition in America—including local activists, community organizers, church groups, labor unions, and minorities—must take foreign policy issues more seriously than they have. Without some curtailment of cold war rhetoric, there simply will not be any advances in affirmative action, community control over economic development, labor union organizing, or any other such issue. And secondly it means that the peace groups and anti-militarist organizations which have been concerned with foreign policy need to combine a preoccupation with moral witness and individual conscience with a larger political understanding of the world that illustrates why militarism has become such a crucial aspect of American politics. When both of these changes occur, a solid basis for an anti-militarist coalition will be laid.

86

Such a coalition has at the present time a major opportunity to develop a program that would have overwhelming popular support in the United States. Unlike all previous peaks of the Soviet threat, the third upturn that began after 1976 comes at a time when the economy is in a state of fairly permanent stagnation. This means that the United States simply cannot afford what its alleged protectors will demand. Moreover, if belt-tightening is achieved in order to increase U.S. rearmament, the longterm economic consequences would be extraordinarily severe. Whatever "security" the American people would feel by having Trident submarines and M-X missiles would in no time be undermined by the inflation, poor economic performance, and balance-of-payments problems that would directly follow from building them. There is a big difference between spending money on arms when it seems to stimulate economic growth and spending money on arms when there is very little money around. The cold warriors are more economically vulnerable in the late 1970s than they have ever been.

But economic vulnerability will not be turned into an asset for those who want to see a secure and stable future for the United States unless they are able to expand their program into one that has mass appeal. To this point, that battle is not being won. The new cold warriors, like the advertising industry, has been adept at exploiting personal insecurities in order to sell their product. Their hysterical campaign to convince the American people that a threat to security exists has won converts, even though most people cannot articulate the nature of the threat they feel. Yet the issue has not been resolved. Most public opinion polls show that no strong and unbreakable support exists for increasing the defense budget and that the Strategic Arms Limitation Treaty with the Soviets is still popular among the American people. There is no *prima facie* reason why a program that emphasizes peace cannot be so appealing that it will drive the Soviet threat out of Washington for good.

A massive peace campaign could take heart from the kinds of issues addressed in this report. I have tried to show how, time after time, elites that possessed extremely unpopular ideas—such as a strong executive, an expensive public sector, an inflationary program, an emphasis on large-scale production, and a demand for domestic sacrifice to stabilize the world economy—have managed to stifle the strong opposition to their vision by manipulating the Soviet threat. The task, then, is to try to take off the husk of the Soviet threat, which does have mass appeal, so that the kernel of an undemocratic and monopolistic economic program, which does not, will be revealed.

As America chooses between a narrow and nasty retreat into selfishness and an opportunity to restructure itself so as to face the future with its humanity and tolerance intact, few questions will be more important than that of the Soviet threat.

To raise the issue of the Soviet threat, therefore, is to raise questions about the whole direction that the American political system has taken since the New Deal. It is to ask questions like these:

- Do we need a presidency so strong that all other political institutions in America, including political parties, legislative bodies, and dissenting traditions wither?
- What have been the costs of relying on a governing coalition that has sought to secure such a firm place in the center of the political spectrum that it has stifled public debate, contributed to an apolitical cynicism, and enabled policymakers to satisfy their self interest without public scrutiny?
- If a free-trade world order demands that we accept unemployment due to the export of jobs, declining productivity and innovation at home, and the use of the dollar to facilitate world trade, have the costs of relying on worldwide economic growth become too expensive for the American people?
- Do we need to rely on an economy that organizes itself from the top down, restricts competition, and finances its growth through inflationary and inefficient boondoggles like the military budget?
- Can we afford to allow the protectors of our security, especially the military services and all the constituents that surround them, to protect themselves against each other by passing the costs on to everyone else?

The answers to these questions are not obvious. There are times and situations where strong leadership may be necessary. One should not necessarily cut oneself off from the world economy. Sometimes inflation has to be accepted in order to achieve other goals. Competitive capitalism is not in itself a good thing, especially if it exploits labor, as it tends to do. But these are issues that the American people need to discuss, and so long as the Soviet threat dominates the political agenda, they are issues

88

that probably will not be discussed.

As the 1980s come upon us, America seems uncertain of itself. Its political future is clouded. There is an air of unpredictability about its role in the world. Its discourse has begun to turn ugly. There is a general feeling throughout the land that something has gone wrong, that the dream has been spoiled. Prophets of doom and withdrawal abound. At the same time, all of those forces that stand for decency, fairness, and peace have begun to arouse themselves from a prolonged stupor. There is a sense of movement and change, a feeling that the current impasse is as much an opportunity as a possible debacle. As America chooses between a narrow and nasty retreat into selfishness and an opportunity to restructure itself so as to face the future with its humanity and tolerance intact, few questions will be more important than that of the Soviet threat. If Americans wake up to the danger posed from those within their midst who would destroy the best features of their country in order to militarize it against an illusory enemy, they have a chance to create the kind of future that they will then deserve.

Footnotes

1. Committee on the Present Danger, *Common Sense and the Present Danger,* p. 2. Cited in Alan Wolfe and Jerry Sanders, "Resurgent Cold War Ideology: The Case of the Committee on the Present Danger," in Richard Fagen (ed.), *Capital and the State in U.S.-Latin American Relations* (Stanford: Stanford University Press, 1979).

2. Committee on the Present Danger, *What is the Soviet Union Up To?,* p. 10; Lt. Gen. Daniel Graham in *United States/Soviet Strategic Options,* Hearings before the Senate Foreign Relations Subcommittee on Arms Control, Oceans, and International Environment, 95th Congress, First Session (1977), p. 123. Both cited in Les Aspin, "What are the Russians Up To?" *International Security* (Summer 1978), p. 30.

3. Aspin, p. 42.

4. *Ibid.,* p. 49.

5. See the Boston Study Group, *The Price of Defense, A New Strategy for Military Spending* (New York: New York Times Books, 1979).

6. Michael T. Klare, "The 'Power Projection' Gap," *The Nation* (June 9, 1979), p. 671.

7. The theme of Soviet-American cooperation is more fully developed in Alan Wolfe, "SALT and the U.S.-Soviet Alliance," *The Nation* (June 23, 1979), p. 737; and Mary Kaldor, *The Disintegrating West* (London: Allen Lane, 1978).

8. George Kistiakowsky, "False Alarm Over SALT," *New York Review of Books* (March 22, 1979), pp. 33-38.

9. Daniel Yergin, *Shattered Peace* (Boston: Houghton Mifflin Co., 1978), pp. 17-68.

10. Cited in *Ibid.,* p. 82.

11. *Idem.*

12. *Ibid.,* p. 83.

13. An interesting treatment of these men is contained in Martin Weil, *A Pretty Good Club* (New York: W.W. Norton & Co., Inc., 1978).

14. NSC-68, which was declassified in 1975, is reprinted in Thomas H. Etzold and John Lewis Gaddis (eds.), *Containment: Documents on American Policy and Strategy, 1945-1950* (New York: Columbia University Press, 1978), pp. 385-442.

15. Dean Acheson, *Present at the Creation* (New York: W.W. Norton & Co., Inc., 1969), p. 374.

16. John Lewis Gaddis, *Russia, the Soviet Union, and the United States* (New York: John Wiley and Sons, Inc., 1978), p. 207.

17. *Ibid.,* p. 209.

18. Walter Lafeber, *America, Russia, and the Cold War, 1945-66* (New York: John Wiley and Sons, Inc., 1967), pp. 209-210.

19. Samuel P. Huntington, *The Common Defense* (New York: Columbia University Press. 1961), p. 87. Huntington points out the difference between

NSC-68 and the New Look: the former was a national *security* policy, the latter only a national policy. For this reason, the Eisenhower Administration rarely exaggerated Soviet military strength, as later administrations were to do: "Administration leaders frequently deprecated Soviet capabilities, particularly in airpower . . . " (p. 69).

20. *Ibid.,* p. 95.

21. These figures are calculated from Barry M. Blechman and Stephen S. Kaplan, *Force Without War: U.S. Armed Forces as a Political Instrument* (Washington: Brookings Institution, 1978), pp. 547-553.

22. *Deterrence and Survival in the Nuclear Age (The "Gaither Report of 1957"),* prepared for the use of the Joint Committee on Defense Production, Congress of the United States (Washington: U.S. Government Printing Office, 1976).

23. Maxwell Taylor, *The Uncertain Trumpet* (New York: Harper and Row Pub., Inc., 1960).

24. Henry Kissinger, *Nuclear Weapons and Foreign Policy* (New York: Harper and Row, Pub., Inc., 1957).

25. For critical assessments of Kennedy's foreign policy adventurism, see Richard J. Walton, *Cold War and Counterrevolution: The Foreign Policy of JFK* (New York: Viking Press, 1972) and Louise FitzSimmons, *The Kennedy Doctrine* (New York: Random House, Inc., 1972).

26. Kennedy's penchant for crises is dissected in Henry Fairlie, *The Kennedy Promise: The Politics of Expectation* (Garden City: Doubleday & Co., Inc., 1973).

27. Lafeber, p. 202.

28. William Shawcross, *Sideshow: Kissinger, Nixon and the Destruction of Cambodia* (New York: Simon and Schuster, Inc., 1979).

29. For the details of how Nixon won approval for SALT I from the Pentagon and Senate, see John Newhouse, *Cold Dawn* (New York: Holt, Rinehart and Winston, 1973).

30. Henry A. Kissinger, *American Foreign Policy* (Third Edition; New York: W.W. Norton & Co., Inc., 1974), pp. 89, 59.

31. Calculated from *Economic Report of the President,* transmitted to the Congress, January, 1978 (Washington: U.S. Government Printing Office, 1978), p. 257.

32. Blechman and Kaplan, *op cit.*

33. Cited in Wolfe and Sanders, *op cit.*

34. Richard Pipes, "Why the Soviet Union Thinks It Could Fight a Nuclear War and Win," *Commentary 64* (July 1977), pp. 21-34.

35. Interview with Wolfe and Sanders. Cited in *op cit.*

36. *Ibid.*

37. Marshall D. Shulman, "Overview of U.S.-Soviet Relations," The Department of State, *Statement,* October 26, 1977.

38. *New York Times,* January 6, 1978, p. A4.

39. Here is Carter speaking:

"There are . . . times when there is no single overwhelming crisis—yet profound national interests are at stake.

"At such times the risks of inaction can be . . . great. It becomes the task of leaders to call forth the vast and restless energies of our people to build for the future.

"That is what Harry Truman did in the years after the Second World War when we helped Europe and Japan rebuild themselves and secured an international order that has protected freedom from aggression.

"We live in such times now—and face such duties." *New York Times,* January 20, 1978, p. A12.

40. *New York Times,* June 8, 1978.

41. For a detailed examination of cold war liberalism, see Alan Wolfe *America's Impasse* (New York: Pantheon Books, Inc., forthcoming).

42. Barton J. Berstein, "Economic Policies," in Richard S. Kirkendall (ed.) *The Truman Period as a Research Field* (Columbia, Mo.: University of Missouri Press, 1967).

43. For an account of anti-communist liberalism see Mary Sperling McAuliffe *Crisis on the Left: Cold War Politics and American Liberals, 1947-54* (Amherst, Mass.: University of Massachusetts Press, 1978).

44. Kevin Phillips, *The Emerging Republican Majority* (New York: Arlington House, Inc., 1969).

45. See Samuel P. Huntington, *Political Order in Changing Society* (New Haven: Yale University Press, 1968), pp. 98-138.

46. On the increasing role of the state in the twentieth century, see Gabriel Kolko, *Main Currents in American History* (New York: Harper and Row Pub., Inc., 1976).

47. Bert Cochran, *Harry Truman and the Crisis Presidency* (New York: Funk and Wagnalls, Inc., 1973).

48. Yergin, pp. 282-83.

49. *Ibid.,* p. 351.

50. Arthur M. Schlesinger, Jr., *A Thousand Days* (Greenwich, Conn.: Fawcett Books, 1965), p. 117.

51. Richard P. Nathan, *The Plot that Failed: Nixon and the Administrative Presidency* (New York: John Wiley and Sons, Inc., 1975).

52. Joseph A. Califano, Jr., *A Presidential Nation* (New York: W.W. Norton & Co., Inc., 1975), p. 11.

53. Blechman and Kaplan, pp. 119-123,

54. On the background to these debates see Demetrios Caraley, *The Politics of Military Unification* (New York: Columbia University Press, 1966); and Robert Borosage, "The Making of the National Security State," in Leonard S. Rodberg and Derek Shearer (eds.), *The Pentagon Watchers* (Garden City: Anchor Books, 1970), pp. 3-63.

55. Morris Janowitz, *Social Control of the Welfare State* (New York: Elsevier North-Holland, Inc., 1976), p. 37.

56. President's Air Policy Commission, *Survival in the Air Age* (Washington: U.S. Government Printing Office, 1948).

57. Cited in Yergin, p. 341.

58. Franz Schurman, *The Logic of World Power* (New York: Pantheon Books, Inc., 1974), p. 154.

59. Taylor, *op cit.*

60. On the Asia-first outlook see Thomas McCormick, *China Market: America's Quest for Informal Empire* (Chicago: Quadrangle, 1967). The distinction between Asia-firsters and Europhiles is similar to Schurman's distinction between expansionists and imperialists. See Schurman, pp. 4-30.

61. On the Europeanist inclinations behind the Marshall Plan see Fred L. Block, *The Origins of International Economic Disorder* (Berkeley and Los Angeles: University of California Press, 1977), pp. 70-108.

62. For details on this period, see Richard M. Freeland, *The Truman Doctrine and the Origins of McCarthyism* (New York: Schocken Books, Inc., 1974).

63. Block, pp. 114-137.

64. Jim F. Heath, *Decade of Disillusionment: The Kennedy-Johnson Years* (Bloomington: Indiana University Press, 1975). Heath notes why Kennedy decided to make a stand over Berlin: "Being tough in foreign affairs was an effective technique for shutting off right-wing criticism, and, politically, he could afford to do so because the disorganized left and the independent liberals had no alternative but to support his administration." (p. 89).

65. I recall, as a teenager, how the Berlin Wall became a symbol of all the evils of communism. Yet in retrospect, a wall is more a symbol of the bankruptcy of the Soviet system, not its expansion. What could be more self-revealing than this attempt to shut off experience from a presumed social revolution?

66. Schlesinger, *A Thousand Days*, p. 541.

67. This point has been made by a number of Marxist critics, especially Samir Amin, *Accumulation on a World Scale* (New York: Monthly Review Press, 1974).

68. W.W. Rostow, *The Stages of Economic Growth* (Second edition; Cambridge: Cambridge University Press, 1971), p. 164.

69. Kissinger, p. 105.

70. Leslie Gelb and Richard Bates, *The Irony of Vietnam: The System Worked* (Washington: Brookings Institution, 1979).

71. See Holly Sklar (ed.), *Trilateralism: Elite Planning for World Management* (Boston: South End Press, forthcoming).

72. Paul Baran and Paul Sweezy, *Monopoly Capitalism* (New York: Monthly Review Press, 1967).

73. Seymour Melman, *The Permanent War Economy* (New York: Simon and Schuster Inc., 1974).

74. James O'Connor, "The Meaning of Economic Imperialism," in Robert I. Rhodes (ed.), *Imperialism and Underdevelopment: A Reader* (New York: Monthly Review Press, 1970), pp. 101-150. See S.M. Miller *et al,* "Does the U.S. Economy Require Imperialism?" *Social Policy* 1 (September-October 1970),

pp. 12-19 for a critique of this point of view.

75. Etzkold and Gaddis, *Containment.*

76. Arthur Schlesinger, Jr., *Robert Kennedy and His Times* (Boston: Houghton Mifflin Co., 1978), p. 407.

77. For an analysis of Carter's use of the defense budget see Gordon Adams and David A. Gold, "Carter's New Cold War Coalition," *The Nation* (February 17, 1979), p. 168.

78. See Richard Burt, "MX Missile Could Mark Big Switch in U.S. Nuclear Policy," *New York Times,* June 16, 1979, p. 5.

IPS Publications

The Politics of National Security
By Marcus G. Raskin

This historical analysis of the national security state traces its evolution from a planning instrument to ensure national stability, mute class conflicts and secure the domestic economy to the basis for covert and overt imperialism. The debacle in Indochina, the genocidal nature of the arms race, and growing economic instability, however, signal the decline of this structure. This incisive study impels renewed public debate of national policy and purpose. $5.95.

Peace in Search of Makers
Riverside Church Reverse the Arms Race Convocation
Jane Rockman, Editor

A compilation of papers denouncing the proliferation of sophisticated weaponry, which threatens a nuclear cataclysm and destroys our society by diverting resources from social services and programs. This volume confronts the moral, economic, strategic and ethical aspects of the arms race and appeals for a citizen coalition to reverse the course of social decay and uncontrolled nuclear armament. Contributions by Richard Barnet, Michael Klare, Cynthia Arnson, Marcus Raskin and others. $5.95.

NEWLY REVISED!

The Counterforce Syndrome:
A Guide to U.S. Nuclear Weapons and Strategic Doctrine
By Robert C. Aldridge

An identification of how "counterforce" has replaced "deterrence" as the Pentagon's prevailing doctrine, contrary to what most Americans believe. This thorough summary and analysis of U.S. strategic nuclear weapons and military doctrine includes descriptions of MIRVs, MARVs, Trident systems, cruise missiles, and M-X missiles as they relate to the aims of a U.S. first strike. $3.95.

The Giants
Russia and America
By Richard Barnet

An authoritative, comprehensive account of the latest stage of the complex U.S.-Soviet relationship; how it came about, what has changed, and where it is headed.

"A thoughtful and balanced account of American-Soviet relations. Barnet goes beyond current controversies to discuss the underlying challenges of a relationship that is crucial to world order." — Cyril E. Black, Director, Center for International Studies, Princeton University

"An extraordinarily useful contribution to the enlightenment of the people of this country . . . . It is of fundamental importance that we understand the true state of our relations with Russia if we are to avoid a tragic mistake in our future." — Senator J.W. Fulbright. $3.95.

Dubious Specter:
A Second Look at the 'Soviet Threat'
By Fred Kaplan

A thorough exposition and analysis of the myths and realities surrounding the current U.S.-Soviet "military balance." Kaplan's comparisons of U.S. and Soviet nuclear arsenals and strategies provide the necessary background for understanding current debates on arms limitations and rising military costs. $2.95.

NEWLY REVISED!

The Rise and Fall of the 'Soviet Threat':
Domestic Sources of the Cold War Consensus
By Alan Wolfe

A timely essay which demonstrates that American fear of the Soviet Union tends to fluctuate due to domestic factors, not in relation to the military and foreign policies of the USSR. Wolfe contends that recurring features of American domestic politics periodically coalesce to spur anti-Soviet sentiment, contributing to increased tensions and dangerous confrontations. $3.95.

Resurgent Militarism
By Michael T. Klare
and the Bay Area Chapter of the Inter-University Committee

An analysis of the origins and consequences of the growing militaristic fervor which is spreading from Washington across the nation. The study examines America's changing strategic position since Vietnam and the political and economic forces which underlie the new upsurge in militarism. $2.00.

Toward World Security:
A Program for Disarmament
By Earl C. Ravenal

This proposal argues that in light of destabilizing new strategic weapons systems and increasing regional conflicts which could involve the superpowers, the U.S. should take independent steps toward disarmament by not deploying new "counterforce" weapons, pledging no first use of nuclear weapons, and by following a non-interventionist foreign policy. $2.00.

Conventional Arms Restraint:
An Unfulfilled Promise
By Michael T. Klare and Max Holland

A review of several aspects of current steps to reduce the amounts and sophistication of weapons sold, close loopholes in Carter administration policy on overall sales, especially to human rights violators, reduce secrecy, improve Congressional oversight, limit co-production arrangements and restrict sales of police and related equipment to authoritarian regimes abroad. $2.00.

Myths and Realities of the 'Soviet Threat'
Proceedings of an IPS Conference on U.S.-Soviet Relations

Distinguished experts explore the prospect for change in the USSR, define the role of the Soviet military in Eastern Europe and assess the U.S.-Soviet military balance. Based on reliable data and analytical rigor, these statements debunk the myth of a new Soviet threat. $2.00.

The New Generation of Nuclear Weapons
By Stephen Daggett

An updated summary of strategic weapons, including American and Soviet nuclear hardware. These precarious new technologies may provoke startling shifts in strategic policy, leading planners to consider fighting "limited nuclear wars" or consider a preemptive first strike capability. $.75.

Supplying Repression:
U.S. Support for Authoritarian Regimes Abroad
By Michael T. Klare

A description of how the U.S. continues to supply arms and training to police and other internal security forces of repressive governments abroad. "Very important, fully documented indictment of U.S. role in supplying rightist Third World governments with the weaponry and know-how of repression." — *The Nation*. $2.95.

South Africa:
Foreign Investment and Apartheid
By Lawrence Litvak, Robert DeGrasse, Kathleen McTigue

A critical examination of the argument that multinationals and foreign investment are a force for progressive change in South Africa. This study carefully documents the role that foreign investment has played in sustaining apartheid. $3.95.

Black South Africa Explodes
By Counter Information Services

The only detailed account available of events in South Africa in the first year since the uprising which began in June 1976 in Soweto. The report exposes the reality of life in the African townships, the impact of South Africa's economic crisis on blacks, and the white regime's dependence on European and American finance. $2.95.

Buying Time in South Africa
By Counter Information Services

An update of events in South Africa since 1976. Despite a severe recession, continuing struggle and external criticism, the South African state has reaffirmed and increased its control. Supported by world banks, multinationals and governments with an economic stake in South Africa, the racist regime is implementing the "grand apartheid" by eliminating all blacks through the creation of home states. $2.95.

The Sullivan Principles:
Decoding Corporate Camouflage
By Elizabeth Schmidt

An analysis of the Sullivan Principles, the fair employment code devised by American corporations in South Africa to deflect public criticism of investment in that country. Demonstrates that even corporations pledged to these principles inevitably bolster the white minority regime with capital, technology and know-how. $1.50.

After the Shah
By Fred Halliday

The sources and nature of the opposition to the Shah of Iran are examined in this paper. Important background information on the National Front, the Tudeh Party, the religious opposition and many other groups. Now that the Shah has been forced to leave the country, Iran's future will be determined by the policies and programs of the disparate groups surveyed here. $2.00.

Feeding the Few:
Corporate Control of Food
By Susan George

The author of *How the Other Half Dies* has extended her critique of the world food system which is geared toward profit not people. This study draws the links between the hungry at home and those abroad exposing the economic and political forces pushing us towards a unified global food system. $3.95.

From Seed to Stomach
A Critique of the U.S. Food System
By Eleanor LeCain

This study traces recent developments in American agriculture, outlining trends in the food production, marketing and distribution/consumption stages. The author shows how the increasing corporate control of food is undermining the productive capacity of the world's largest food producer. $3.95.

The Crisis of the Corporation
By Richard Barnet

Now a classic, this essay analyzes the power of the multinational corporations which dominate the U.S. economy, showing how the growth of multinationals inevitably results in an extreme concentration of economic and political power in a few hands. The result, according to Barnet, is a crisis for democracy itself. $1.50.

The New Gnomes:
Multinational Banks in the Third World
By Howard M. Wachtel

This work documents and analyzes the growth of Third World debt to private U.S.-based multinational banks, and the impact of this new form of indebtedness on the politics and economic policies of Third World countries. $3.95.

'Til Death Do Us Part:
The American Nuclear Power Industry
By Mark Hertsgaard

A profile of the political economy of the U.S. nuclear industry. The study details the massive subsidy provided for the development of nuclear power; describes the corporations involved and their strategies for the future. A must for understanding the future debate on nuclear power. $6.95.

The Nuclear Disaster
By Counter Information Services

An analysis of Great Britain's nuclear power industry. A history of government mismanagement, secrecy and subsidized profits for private energy monopolies is contrasted with the dismal record of the nuclear power industry regarding escalating prices, declining job creation, and health dangers from radiation and nuclear waste disposal. An appendix profiling nuclear companies, state regulating agencies, U.K. reactor orders, and a chronology of nuclear power is included. $2.95.

The Ford Report
By Counter Information Services

This "anti-report" by CIS, a London affiliate of the Institute for Policy Studies, is a comprehensive and well-documented study on the Ford Motor Company. The report deals with Ford activities in South Africa, its role in the Common Market, its plans for the Third World, wages and working conditions, death on the job, profits and production, and Ford's blueprint for the future. $2.95.

Chile:
Economic 'Freedom' and Political Repression
By Orlando Letelier

A dramatic analysis by the former leading official of the Allende government who was assassinated by the Pinochet junta. This essay demonstrates the necessary relationship between an economic development model which benefits only the wealthy few and the political terror which has reigned in Chile since the overthrow of the Allende regime. $1.00.

Human Rights, Economic Aid and Private Banks:
The Case of Chile
By Michael Moffitt and Isabel Letelier

This issue paper documents the tremendous increase in private bank loans to the Chilean military dictatorship since the overthrow of Salvador Allende in 1973. Previously unpublished data demonstrates how private banks rescued the Chilean military government by increasing loans to Chile at the very time governments and international institutions were reducing their loans because of massive human rights violations. $2.00.

The Links Between Struggles for Human Rights in the United States and the Third World
By Congressman Ron Dellums

The keynote address at the 1978 Letelier-Moffitt Human Rights Memorial. Stating that human rights violations stem from the system, not the individual, he calls for a powerful coalition of all minorities, Third World people and progressive human beings to change America and the world. $.50.

The First Americans:
Fighting for a Future to Inherit the Past
By Pablo Letelier and Judy L. Ziegler

An account of the Mapuche's struggle against the policies which threaten the extinction of all indigenous groups in Chile. This indictment of the Chilean military regime is the first in a series designed to document the historical and current exploitation and human rights violations of Native Americans. $1.95.

Whistle-Blowers Guide to the Federal Bureaucracy
By Government Accountability Project

This handbook was written to aid employees of the federal government who need to reach the public with evidence of illegal or improper practices in their agencies. Based on the experience of such veterans as Ernie Fitzgerald, it tells prospective whistleblowers the consequences to expect and how to afford themselves maximum protection. $3.00.

Public Employee Pension Funds:
New Strategies for Investment
By Lee Webb and William Schweke

A guide detailing channels for redirecting public pension fund assets to socially useful investments. This work surveys legal questions, portfolio management, political and institutional obstacles and alternative investment opportunities. Including a bibliography and glossary of financial terms, this volume is essential for public officials and employee unions, economic development specialists and public interest groups. $9.95/$14.95 institutions.

Tax Abatements:
Resources for Public Officials and Community Leaders
By Ed Kelly and Lee Webb

A current examination of tax abatements which favor corporations with special deals while increasing onerous local property taxes. Attributing the problem to corporate influence on local government, this analysis identifies the tactics successfully employed by public officials, community groups and labor unions to thwart corporate parasitism. $4.95/$6.95 institutions.

Plant Closings:
Resources for Public Officials and Community Leaders
Ed Kelly and Lee Webb, Editors

A comprehensive resource manual detailing the problems of plant closings and runaway shops. This collection of essays, magazine articles, policy reports and press clips outlines the causes of plant closings and prescribes organizing and legislative strategies to prevent them. Indispensible for union leaders, public officials, academics and community activists. $4.95/$6.95 institutions.

State and Local Tax Reform
Perspective, Proposal and Resources
Dean Tipps and Lee Webb, Editors

A comprehensive guide to state and local tax issues. Progressive tax experts discuss both the problems of tax equity and the prospects for reform initiatives, emphasizing property, estate and sales taxes and innovative proposals for taxing land speculation, business and corporate profits. This compendium includes original articles, material from periodicals, leaflets, and memos prepared in tax reform campaigns. $9.95/$14.95 institutions.

Public Policy for the 80's:
Perspectives and Resources for State and Local Action
Lee Webb, Editor

The definitive guide to public policy issues for the 80's. This handbook offers rigorous analysis of controversies in energy, economic development, state and local tax reform and agriculture. Focusing on 27 critical issues facing state and local governments, nationally recognized experts present extensive resource information on organizations, individuals and publications for policymaking in the 80's. $9.95/$14.95 institutions.

Postage and Handling:
All orders must be prepaid. For delivery within the USA, please add 15% of order total. For delivery outside the USA, add 20%. Standard discounts available upon request.

Please write the Institute for Policy Studies, 1901 Que Street, N.W., Washington, D.C. 20009 for our complete catalog of publications and films.